stacks

The Art of
Vertical Food

stacks

The Art of Vertical Food

DEBORAH FABRICANT

Ten Speed Press
Berkeley, California

To Julia Child,

whose wit, wisdom, and

knowledge inspired me

1🅢 Ten Speed Press
P.O. Box 7123
Berkeley, California 94707
www.tenspeed.com

Distributed in Australia by Simon & Schuster Australia, in
Canada by Ten Speed Press Canada, in New Zealand by
Southern Publishers Group, in South Africa by Real Books,
in Southeast Asia by Berkeley Books, and in the United
Kingdom and Europe by Airlift Books.

Cover and text design by Catherine Jacobes
Photography by Frankie Frankeny, San Francisco
Food preparation and styling by Wesley Martin, San Francisco,
and Deborah Fabricant

Library of Congress Cataloging-in-Publication Data
Fabricant, Deborah
      Stacks : the art of vertical food / Deborah Fabricant.
            p.cm.
      Includes bibliographical references and index.
      ISBN 1-58008-062-6
      1. Food presentation. 2. Cookery. I. Title.
      TX652.F33   1999   99-20260
      641.5--dc21   CIP

First printing, 1999
Printed in Hong Kong
2 3 4 5 6 7 8 9 10 - 03 02 01 00 99

Contents

ACKNOWLEDGMENTS

To Mary Fitzgerald, my agent, for being in the alley at the right time, for having the patience to help a new author, and for being a tireless one-woman cheering section. Without you, I would not be writing this acknowledgment, because it all began with you.

To my wonderful daughter Samantha and her husband John, who is the son I never had, thank you for everything.

To Mike, the "King Taster," who so willingly ate stack recipes for dinner every night until I had tested them all, who kept up the encouragement and saw me through a lot of changes.

To Henny, my love always. To Lisa, Jessica, Jose, Derek, Scott, and Sara, just because you are who you are and I love you. No matter what.

To John Jolliffe, for telling me to write bold, break out of the mold, and believe in who I really am.

To Gordon and Jill Hally, for their encouragement and their kind gift of a quiet place to gather my thoughts and write.

To Ron Sanchez and Tom Cramer for "table offs," and to Ron for having that fateful birthday.

To my sister Valerie and hubby Frank—a great big thank you!

To Judy Jackson for believing in me since we were in seventh grade. You are a gift!

To the guinea pigs: Alan and Gail Borsari, the Newport Workout gang, and the girls.

To the cheering section: Dale Brown, Pat Parrish, Judy Schoenfeld, Pat Cochran, Julia Gold, Karen Betson, Connie Murphy, Vicki Pouré, Lynn Lieberman, and Lenno Wells.

To Frankie and Wesley for the stunning photography and new friendship.

To Gay Rodriguez, secretary of the universe. You have the ability, patience, and talents of twenty. Thank you. Thank you.

To Deborah Hefter from Envelopment in Irvine, California, for her unsurpassed design ideas for the proposal—you always make it fabulous.

To my friends at Bristol Farms, the Culinary Institute of America at Greystone, Sur La Table, Farmers Market, Surfas, and Cost Plus.

To the wonderful people at Ten Speed Press: Thanks to Phil Wood—love that man—for being in the booth at the Los Angeles Book Festival so I could meet him and feed him stacks; to Lorena Jones, editor, sounding board, and friend, for her insight and talent; to Jo Ann Deck, for tasting and approving; and to Dennis Hayes, for the introduction to Phil Wood. To Chelsea Vaughn for stepping in and carrying the ball. To Catherine Jacobes for doing such a fabulous job in designing the book. To Patti Oien, Amy Cleary, and Anna Erickson for the great publicity job.

To the Higher Power, who led me to this point, keeps me in the groove, and without whom nothing is possible.

Introduction

OVER THE YEARS, I have established a fierce but friendly entertaining competition with my dear friend Ron Sanchez and his partner Tom Cramer. When we visit one another's homes for dinner, we invariably whisk past the host to check out the table, setting, and flowers, eventually ending up in the kitchen, snooping around and lifting lids. We are sneaky, incorrigible, and curious. We also love each other immensely, and our game, all in good fun, is a product of that affection.

Recently, it was Ron's birthday and my turn for a spin in the kitchen. After poring over menus, scanning favorite books, and considering his likes and dislikes, I came up with the perfect idea. I decided to create a stacked salad that was layered in a pipe or cylinder. I spent days searching for the cylinder forms. My resourcefulness was tested, but I came up with the perfect mold—a cylinder crafted from PVC pipe—and went on to make my stacked salad.

When Ron arrived that night, he headed straight for the table to critique the setting and decor. He then made his way into the kitchen, where he saw my "stacked" PVC cylinders carefully placed on Depression-era glass plates. "What's this?" he said. I explained that it was the first course and that I would remove the cylinders before serving. Ron said, "Oh no, you must serve them that way." I told him I thought that would be silly, but he insisted. I finally agreed and dinner was served—cylinders and all. My guests eyed the cylinders with obvious trepidation, and then followed my direction to lift the pipe molds straight up, revealing their stacked first course. When I saw their disbelief and delight, I knew it was just the beginning of stacks for home chefs.

Our guests didn't believe me when I told them the stacks were easy to make. I realized how important it is for home chefs to be able to duplicate the fancy, involved recipes served in great restaurants, and that most "gourmet" recipes are too complicated for home chefs. How often have you had a dinner party, looked through your many cookbooks, and ended up making something familiar, something easy? Don't you often wish you had turned your meal into something more extraordinary? Well, me too—and that is why I wrote this book.

Certainly, many professional chefs use this architectural technique of assembling food. But my stack recipes are specially created for home chefs like you, who are always looking for new ways to keep cooking and entertaining interesting and fun. With these stacks, you will dazzle guests, surprise the kids, eat "skinny food" that looks and tastes sensational, and have a good time in the process.

Always select your ingredients with an eye on freshness and quality. And allow yourself the sweet indulgence of eating the best you can afford. Like many cooks, I learned the principles of good cooking from Julia Child, who taught me that a spoonful of the very best is far better than a whole bowlful of something second-rate. When it's time to sit down to a well-prepared meal, indulging the senses makes the event memorable.

The presentation is important, but the power of simplicity comes first. The actual stack is the presentation, so all you need is a drizzle of sauce and maybe a sprinkling of garnish. One of the fun aspects of stacks is the color they bring to the table. I love color on a pure white plate. The purple of radicchio with a splash of rich orange nectarine creates a mosaic of texture, color, and taste.

More than anything, your adventures in cooking and entertaining should be rewarding and pleasurable. I am not a professionally trained chef. If I can learn the basics, the flavors, the seasons, and the methods of good cooking, you can too. It only takes a little patience, a lot of desire, and the willingness to experience the disasters as well as the triumphs. As a busy person who loves to entertain, I sincerely hope that this book inspires the same creativity and excitement in you that creating that first stack did for me.

To me, good food is an essential ingredient of the good life. It symbolizes comfort and nurturing, provides an outlet for creative expression, reminds us of life's simple pleasures, and commemorates the major and minor milestones of daily life. Food brings us together for family celebrations, anniversaries, birthdays, picnics, and just to enjoy the good life with the company of our favorite people. And each time you start cooking, remember this: a good meal is at the heart of the home.

Getting Started

EVERY TIME I HAVE MADE STACKS, THEY HAVE CAUSED A STIR, from the hoots and cheers of *The Home and Family Show* television audience to the unrestrained enthusiasm of a woman at the Irvine, California, amphitheater who climbed over five rows of chairs to ask about the Chocolate Bread Pudding Stacks I had served at intermission. With the promise of such rewards in mind, let's walk through the basics of making stacks.

How to Make Your Own Stack Cylinders

One of the most memorable times I made stacks was for a dinner at an event for High Priority, a breast cancer charity I support. My buddies Karen Betson and Connie Murphy helped me create a fabulous dinner, starting with a stacked appetizer. Experimenting with makeshift molds (other than lengths of PVC pipe), we used chicken broth and minestrone soup cans, removing both ends and carefully washing them out. The funniest part of the project was watching Karen try to find eggplants, tomatoes, and onions that were exactly the right diameter to fit in the cans. (Later on, she realized that she could trim any vegetable to make it fit.)

The Resources section, page 169, lists places where you can purchase stack cylinders. Should you wish to make a stack creation without having to purchase cylinders, simply use these various sizes of cans with both ends removed:

- 10-ounce soup can
- 14-ounce soup can
- 15-ounce broth can
- 6-ounce tomato paste can
- 6-ounce tuna can

Using these cans is inexpensive, and they are easily adaptable to the recipes in this book. Just follow these steps:

1. Choose a soup, broth, tomato, or tuna can in the desired size.

2. Remove both ends of the can, empty it, and wash the interior thoroughly with warm soapy water.

3. Remove and discard the labels.

4. Dry the cans well.

5. Spray the insides of the cans with vegetable spray before using.

If you are planning a dinner party, start collecting cans several weeks ahead of time, so you aren't scrambling for them at the last minute. After your party, wash and dry the cans and store them for future use. The cans can be used for cold or hot (oven-heated) stacks. Keep in mind that you will need one cylinder per guest.

Where to Purchase Stack Cylinders and Ring Molds

While using recycled cans is a great way to get started, using commercially made cylinders is definitely easier. Any fine gourmet cookware store or professional cooking equipment store should carry a variety of ring molds in various sizes. If you have difficulty finding molds, you can mail-order them from any of the purveyors listed on page 169. When you call and request the ring molds or tall "pastry rings," specify that you are using them for "vertical food presentation" or "stacked food presentation." If you choose to buy the cylinders, you may want to experiment with the following sizes:

■ Small (for appetizers and tiny tea sandwiches): 2 inches in diameter by 3 inches high

■ Medium (for salads, sweets, and starters): 3 inches in diameter by 3 inches high

■ Large (for entrées, salads, sandwiches, and sweets): 3 inches in diameter by 4 inches high

■ Other shapes such as pyramids, squares, and ovals add variety to your collection.

Equipment You Will Need

In addition to your stack cylinders, you will need a few basic pieces of equipment:

- Two 12 by 17-inch sheet pans

- Measuring spoons

- A soup spoon

- A small (1$^1/_2$-ounce) ladle

- Parchment paper or waxed paper

- Long, narrow tongs

- An empty 3-inch-diameter can or jar for compressing the layers (or you can use the backs of your fingers and knuckles, like a real chef)

- Nonstick vegetable spray

- Sharp knives

- Clear plastic wrap (for pyramid molds)

Stack Portions

Stacks are very adaptable. Most of the recipes in this book make six stacks, but if you want smaller or larger portions, it is easy to adjust the recipes. Simply cut or increase the amount of ingredients you put in each layer. If the recipe calls for 3 tablespoons of risotto and you want to make smaller stacks, just layer in 1$^1/_2$ tablespoons, making sure the previous layer is covered. Or you could beef up a salad to make it an entrée salad—a great summer entertaining idea.

As a rule of thumb, each layer should be made with 2 to 3 tablespoons of an ingredient. Some recipes will call for less in one of the layers—usually because that layer is highly flavored and would overpower the others or is used to enhance the overall look and taste.

Stack Shapes

For most of the recipes I have used a standard 3 by 4-inch stack cylinder (comparable to a 15-ounce broth can). However, if you want to experiment, use different shapes, such as square tins, pyramids, triangles, and wider, shorter rings. Many of the suppliers on page 169 stock unusual sizes and shapes. Spam cans make great square stacks, and tuna cans are good for a creating starter stacks, side stacks, and bases for a free-form stack. If you want to make tiny, delicate starter or sandwich stacks, use a tomato paste can with both ends removed, or purchase small ring molds.

The secret to unmolding stacks perfectly is in compressing the layers prior to chilling or baking. Pressing down on the layers with firm but gentle pressure adheres them securely to one another. I use either my knuckles, covering them first with a piece of plastic wrap, or a small jar, can, or rounded meat-pounding or espresso device to compress the layers. If the top layer is delicate, just add it at the very end, after you have compacted the previous layers.

Free-form stacks are fun and easy. Try using tortillas, pancakes, crepes, baked puff pastry shapes, baked phyllo triangles, or meringues. To see an example of a free-form stack, check out the Raspberry-Lemon Meringue Stacks (page 144), the Fruited Saint André Stacks (page 30), Avocado, Tomato, and Phyllo Stacks (page 38), Smoked Salmon with Dilled Potato Waffle Stacks (page 28), or Sweet Potato Pancakes with Rock Shrimp (page 78). Flavored waffles, either sweet or savory (with herbs, nuts, cheese, or shredded vegetables), are a great tool for making free-form stacks.

Advance Preparation: The Best Entertaining Technique

One of the very best features of stacks is that most recipes can be made ahead, chilled, and then reheated just before they are served. Chilled stacks can be served right from the refrigerator or freezer—the answer to every busy host's dream!

When making stacks ahead, go easy on sauces. You can always add more before serving. Saucy recipes have a tendency to drain out the bottom, so I simply stack the food and then add more sauce at the end of the baking time or when serving.

For salad stacks, don't add the final greens on top until just before serving. Fill the stack to the next-to-the-last layer and chill. At serving time, toss the last layer of greens with a bit of dressing and add to the top.

Pantry Essentials

Because most stack recipes require a "soft" food to bind the layers together, I've included some suggestions for stocking your pantry. This is particularly helpful if you have leftover meat or vegetables and want to create a stack quickly—a great way to impress unexpected guests.

The soft foods I keep on hand are listed on page 5. This list is just to get you started. Refer also to the Stacks Matrix on page 8. It will give you an abundance of suggestions for flavor, texture, and complementary food pairings. The Stacks Matrix will also help you create stacks from leftovers. Remember, this is supposed to be fun. Be creative!

Using Leftovers

While most of us shy away from leftovers, I have found them to be ideal for stacks. Imagine roasting a chicken on Sunday and creating a beautiful stack with chicken, mushrooms, risotto, and Parmesan cheese for Monday or Tuesday. Or barbecuing a

PANTRY ESSENTIALS

Angel-hair pasta

Beans

Brown rice

Bulgur

Couscous

Cream cheese

Frozen pound cake

Ice cream

Kasha

Oatmeal

Orzo

Pancake batter

5-minute polenta

Potatoes (for mashing)

Risotto

Sundried tomatoes

Sushi rice

Sweet potatoes

Tapioca

Wild rice

*For flavoring and sauces I keep several staples on hand,
knowing they will be frequently used:*

Caramel sauce

Chocolate sauce

Consorzio flavored oils (available in fine
markets and gourmet food shops)

Dijon, honey, sweet, and hot mustards

Garlic

Good extra virgin olive oil

Lemon curd

Parmesan, mozzarella, goat, and
blue cheeses

Pine nuts, walnuts, pecans, almonds

Semisweet chocolate

Tomato or fruit salsa

Vanilla ice cream

Vinegars: flavored, balsamic,
Japanese, wine

flank steak one night and making a stack with the flank steak, asparagus, black bean sauce, and sushi rice the next evening. The possibilities are endless. Not only is using leftovers practical and economical, your perceived cooking skills will earn you raves. Rather than dishing out what is left of yesterday's dinner, you will have created a simple, satisfying work of art.

Shortcut Stacks

You will see Shortcut Stacks notes throughout the book. For the busy person, the tips in these sidebars are invaluable. They tell how to replace made-from-scratch elements of recipes with quality convenience foods—for example, using a bakery angel food cake or brownies instead of homemade ones. The products mentioned are available from fine markets and gourmet food shops, or by ordering from Bristol Farms Markets (see page 170).

How It All Stacks Up

Assembling the stacks in this book is easier than it looks. Just follow these basic techniques when you make the recipes in this book, and your artful creations will turn out every time.

Step 1

Lightly coat the inside of the mold with nonstick vegetable spray and set the mold on the serving plate or baking sheet. Begin layering the ingredients inside the mold, as directed in the recipe, taking care to fit them snugly into the cylinder or mold, creating distinct layers.

Step 2

When the cylinder or mold is filled, press down gently but firmly to compress the layers. This ensures that your stack will hold together when unmolded.

Step 3

When the stack is completed, refrigerate, freeze, or bake as the recipe indicates.

Step 4

To serve, using a wide spatula, transfer the stack to a serving plate. With one hand, gently lift the mold off of the stack of ingredients, using the other hand to steady the stack.

Step 5

Garnish the stack as directed and serve immediately.

Now that you are armed with this information on getting started, you are in for a lot of fun and creativity. Gather your family and friends and stack it all up together. Consider this food art group therapy!

The recipes in this book are just a start. Once you have tried some of the dishes, refer to the Stacks Matrix that follows and try a hand at becoming your own chef. The sky's the limit . . . have fun!

The Stacks Matrix

This comprehensive list of compatible foods will allow you to exercise your creativity and design your own stacks combinations. Read the Matrix from left to right, choosing one "Binder" and any combination of vegetables, seafood, meat, cheeses, fruits, seasonings, and sauces. I have given some favorite flavor combinations in the far right-hand column to guide you. Have fun with this creative process and use your imagination to create your own signature stacks.

	BINDER	VEGETABLES	FISH/MEATS	CHEESES	

Starter Stacks	angel-hair pasta
	blini
	bread
	cellophane noodles
	couscous
	crepes
	mashed beans
	pancakes
	phyllo
	polenta
	potatoes
	  • mashed
	  • sweet
	  • white
		asparagus
		avocados
		corn
		eggplant
		leeks
		mesclun
		mushrooms
		onions
		peppers
		scallions
		tomatoes
		zucchini
			caviar
			chicken
			crab
			duck
			foie gras
			lobster
			mussels
			oysters
			pancetta
			pâté
			prosciutto
			salmon
			sausage
			scallops
			shrimp
			smoked fish
				boursin-pepper
				Brie
				feta
				fontina
				goat cheese/chèvre
				Maytag
				Montrachet
				mozzarella di bufala
				Parmesan
				Port du Salut
				Roquefort
				Saint André
				Stilton	

The Stacks Matrix

FRUITS	SEASONINGS/NUTS	SAUCES/DRESSINGS	FAVORITE COMBINATIONS
apples	almonds	aioli	Blini, caviar, onion, egg
blueberries	basil	garlic	Cellophane noodles with scallops, enoki mushrooms, and ginger
cherries	capers	herbal cream	
cranberries	cayenne	mustards	Tiny crepes with duck, wild mushrooms, and apples
figs	chiles	shallot	
kiwi	chives	sour cream	Truffle mashed potatoes with lobster and caviar
mangoes	cilantro	sundried tomatoes	
melon	cumin	tomato	
peaches	dill	vinaigrettes	
plums	garlic		
raspberries	ginger		
strawberries	nutmeg		
	olives		
	oregano		
	parsley		
	pesto		
	pine nuts		
	rosemary		
	sage		
	thyme		

The Stacks Matrix

Choose one from each column.

	BINDER	VEGETABLES	FISH/MEATS	CHEESES	
Salad Stacks	bread/croutons brown rice couscous crepes lentils mashed potatoes phyllo risotto white rice	artichoke hearts arugula asparagus avocados eggplant endive English cucumbers field greens frisee green beans jicama mesclun onions peppers radicchio radishes red lettuce spinach squash tomatoes	anchovies caviar chicken crab lobster pancetta salmon sardines sausage scallops sea bass shrimp smoked fish turkey	blue cheese Brie Cambozola feta goat cheese/chèvre Gruyère Jack mozzarella mozzarella di bufala Parmesan Saint Agur smoked Gouda	
Seafood Stacks	angel-hair pasta corn pancakes couscous fried wontons lentils mashed potatoes polenta quinoa rice pilaf risotto sushi rice sweet potato pancakes wild rice pancakes	artichoke hearts asparagus avocados baby greens bok choy broccoli chanterelles corn eggplant endive fennel green beans jicama leeks mushrooms peas peppers radicchio ratatouille red cabbage spinach sprouts tomatoes watercress zucchini	bacon caviar crab escolar grilled salmon lobster mussels oysters pancetta prawns prosciutto rock shrimp sardines scallops sea bass skate smoked fish smoked salmon soft-shell crab sole swordfish tuna	Brie feta goat cheese/chèvre Gorgonzola mozzarella di bufala Parmesan ricotta	

FRUITS	SEASONINGS/NUTS	SAUCES/DRESSINGS	FAVORITE COMBINATIONS
apples blood oranges cranberries currants dried apricots dried cherries dried cranberries figs mangoes nectarines papaya pears persimmons pomegranates raisins	basil capers cardamom chives cilantro cumin dill ginger hazelnuts lemon thyme marjoram mustard olives oregano pecans pine nuts pistachios red pepper flakes sesame oil sesame seeds shallots star anise tarragon walnuts watercress	balsamic vinegar fig green chile salsa herb hoisin hot sauce lemon lime mango chutney mustard sesame-ginger soy sundried tomato vinaigrette	Arugula and radicchio, with pears, toasted walnuts, and Gorgonzola Avocado, papaya, and watercress Mushrooms, spinach, Gruyère, and barley Pears, walnuts, frisee, and Parmesan Romaine, blood oranges, walnuts, and feta Shrimp, avocado, and pancetta with pineapple salsa
fruit salsas grapefruit mangoes oranges pineapple watermelon	basil bay leaves black sesame seeds capers chervil chives cilantro dill fennel garlic ginger lemongrass marjoram mustard oregano parsley saffron sesame oil sorrel tarragon thyme wasabi	aioli Asian chile-garlic crème fraîche hoisin horseradish lemon lime orange shallot sorrel cream soy spinach tamari tapenade Thai peanut tomato coulis watercress wine	Grilled shrimp and onions, white rice, and pineapple salsa Lemon angel hair, salmon, and watercress Salmon with lentils, mushrooms, and onions Shrimp, quinoa, and roasted peppers Sushi stacks Sweet potato pancakes with scallops and crispy prosciutto Swordfish with tapenade, couscous, and eggplant

The Stacks Matrix

Choose one from each column.

	BINDER	VEGETABLES	FISH/MEATS	CHEESES	

Savory Stacks	angel-hair pasta
	arborio rice
	barley
	brown rice
	couscous
	garlic mashed
	    potatoes
	grits
	kasha
	lentils
	polenta
	risotto
	spaghetti squash
	sweet mashed
	    potatoes
	tortillas
		artichoke hearts
		avocado
		beans
		carrots
		corn
		eggplant
		endive
		fennel
		field greens
		leeks
		mushrooms
		onions
		peas
		peppers
		roasted garlic
		savoy cabbage
		tomatoes
		truffles
		zucchini
			bacon
			beef
			chicken
			foie gras
			lamb
			pancetta
			pork
			prosciutto
			sausage
			turkey
			veal
				blue cheese
				Brie
				Cheddar
				feta
				Gruyère
				Jack
				mozzarella
				Mozzarella di Bufala
				Parmesan
				ricotta
				Stilton	

Sweet Stacks	angel food cake bread brownies cake cookies crepes custard, thick gingerbread ice cream ladyfingers macaroons meringue mousse oatmeal phyllo pound cake puff pastry rice pudding shortbread sorbet sour cream tapioca, thick waffles			Brie cream cheese goat cheese/chèvre Gorgonzola Gourmandise mascarpone Saint André Stilton	

FRUITS	SEASONINGS/NUTS	SAUCES/DRESSINGS	FAVORITE COMBINATIONS
apples(lamb, pork, chicken)	anchovies	balsamic vinegar	Apricot-spiced lamb with couscous and onions
apricots (lamb, pork, chicken)	basil	barbecue sauce	
cranberries (pork, chicken, turkey)	cayenne	béarnaise	Grilled chicken with basil, sundried tomatoes, eggplant, and polenta
currants	chiles	chile sauce	
dried cherries (lamb, pork, chicken)	chives	cognac	Grilled filet with garlic mashed potatoes, leeks, and porcini wine sauce
oranges (pork, chicken)	cilantro	cream	
plums (lamb, chicken)	cumin	ginger	Sausage, red cabbage, and apple coulis
	curry	horseradish	
	garlic	mustard	Sweet potato mash, grilled chicken, spinach, and roasted garlic
	gremolata	Oriental/soy	
	herb butters	pissirola sauce	
	honey	porcini	
	horseradish	red wine	
	juniper berries	salsa	
	lemon	sour cream	
	marjoram	steak sauce	
	nutmeg	sundried tomato	
	olives	watercress	
	oregano	white wine	
	parsley	Worcestershire sauce	
	pecans		
	pine nuts		
	rosemary		
	saffron		
	sage		
	shallots		
	tarragon		
	thyme		
apples	almonds	caramel	Chocolate brownies with grilled bananas, brown sugar, and chocolate peanut butter sauce
apricots	cardamom	chocolate	
bananas	chocolate	chocolate-peanut butter	
blackberries	cinnamon		
cherries	cloves	chocolate syrup	Fresh peaches, pound cake, and custard with raspberry coulis
dried fruits	coconut	coffee	
figs	ginger	crème fraîche	Orange-glazed figs with almond crepes and mascarpone and praline
kiwis	hazelnuts	fruit salsas	
lemons	mint	fruit sauces	
limes	nutmeg	fruit syrups	Pumpkin, gingerbread, and caramel ice cream
nectarines	pecans	honey	
mangoes	pistachios	liqueurs	Rhubarb and plums with phyllo, peppered crème anglaise, and toasted almonds
oranges	poppy seeds	vanilla sauce	
passion fruit	praline		
peaches	star anise		
pears	streusel		
persimmons	vanilla brown sugar		
pineapple	walnuts		
plums			
pumpkin			
raisins			
raspberries			
strawberries			

Caramelized Onion, Phyllo, Smoked Salmon, and Mesclun Stacks

STARTER STACKS

Caramelized Onion, Phyllo, Smoked Salmon, and Mesclun Stacks

YIELD: 6 SERVINGS

These beautiful free-form stacks can be raised to the utmost elegance with the addition of a dollop of caviar on top, a wonderful choice for a formal luncheon or dinner party.

Planning Ahead

- The caramelized onions can be made up to a week ahead and stored covered in the refrigerator. Reheat before assembling the stacks.
- The phyllo can be made early on the day of preparation.
- Cut the goat cheese and chill.
- Chop the chives and chill.

CARAMELIZED ONIONS

1 tablespoon butter

3 tablespoons extra virgin olive oil

8 large onions, peeled, halved, and sliced

6 large shallots, peeled and sliced

$1/3$ cup balsamic vinegar

$2/3$ cup brown sugar

1 tablespoon chopped chives

PHYLLO

5 tablespoons butter

4 sheets frozen phyllo, thawed

$1/3$ cup minced fresh dill

$2/3$ cup toasted pine nuts (page 161)

6 cups mesclun

2 pounds presliced smoked salmon, about 18 slices

6 slices Montrachet or other goat cheese, $1/8$ inch thick

$1/2$ cup chopped chives

1 teaspoon Osetra caviar, for garnish (optional)

$2/3$ cup lemon vinaigrette (page 158)

Advance Preparation

To make the caramelized onions, heat the butter and the oil in a large skillet until the butter foams, about 1 minute. Do not let the butter burn. Decrease the heat to medium, add the onions and shallots, and cook over low heat until they are translucent, about 15 minutes. Stir in the vinegar and sugar and cook gently for 30 to 45 minutes, or until the vinegar sauce is thick and the onions are caramelized. Watch carefully, stirring occasionally. Stir in the chives and cool to room temperature.

Preheat the oven to 350°.

To make the phyllo, melt the butter in a small saucepan. On a clean work surface, lay out 1 sheet of phyllo. Brush the sheet with butter and sprinkle it with $1^1/_2$ tablespoons dill and 2 tablespoons of pine nuts. Repeat, using all the phyllo sheets. Cut the phyllo into 4-inch squares. Then cut each square crosswise to form two triangles.

Place the triangles on a buttered sheet pan and bake for 8 to 10 minutes, or until golden. Allow the triangles to cool at room temperature.

Assembly

Line 6 serving plates with 1 cup mesclun each, leaving a space in the center for the phyllo. Place 1 phyllo triangle on each plate. Top with a slice of smoked salmon and then 1 tablespoon caramelized onions. Top with another phyllo triangle, placing the points facing in another direction. Top with a slice of cheese, then salmon and onions. Top with the third phyllo triangle, again placing the points in different directions. Top with the third piece of salmon and 1 tablespoon onions.

Garnish with a sprinkle of chives, the caviar, and the remaining pine nuts, drizzle the lettuce with lemon vinaigrette, and serve.

Polenta with Caramelized Pepper Confit and Feta

YIELD: 6 SERVINGS

These were originally 1 inch in diameter rounds of polenta, scooped out in the center and filled with the caramelized peppers. I thought it would be fun to stack them. These can be made in smaller cylinders as hors d'oeuvres; they are colorful, delicious, and hold up very well.

Planning Ahead

- Prepare the polenta rounds the day before and chill.

- Prepare the peppers the day before and chill.

- Assemble the stacks early in the day and chill. Bring to room temperature before baking.

TIP: When peppers are in season, char and peel a bunch. Then place the peppers in plastic bags, label them, and freeze. You will now have "fresh" roasted peppers all year long.

POLENTA ROUNDS

13$^1/_2$ ounces instant polenta

1 tablespoon chopped fresh parsley

3 tablespoons butter, room temperature

1 teaspoon salt

$^1/_2$ teaspoon freshly ground black pepper

1 tablespoon chopped fresh sage

$^1/_2$ cup grated Parmesan cheese

PEPPER CONFIT

4 tablespoons butter

$^1/_2$ pound red bell peppers, seeded and diced

$^1/_2$ pound yellow bell peppers, seeded and diced

3 onions, peeled and diced

4 cloves garlic, minced

1 tablespoon fresh thyme, minced

4 tablespoons brown sugar

Salt and freshly ground black pepper to taste

1 cup dry white wine

$^1/_3$ cup balsamic vinegar

1$^1/_2$ cups crumbled feta cheese

$^1/_2$ cup chopped chives, for garnish

$^1/_2$ cup grated Parmesan cheese, for garnish

Advance Preparation

To make the polenta rounds, prepare the polenta according to package directions.

Add the parsley, butter, salt, pepper, sage, and cheese and stir well. Pour the mixture into a greased 12 by 17-inch sheet pan and smooth evenly. Let set until firm, about 15 minutes.

For entrée stacks, cut the polenta into 12 rounds, each 3 inches in diameter. If making appetizer stacks, cut the polenta into 24 rounds, using a 1-inch cylinder. Set aside.

To make the caramelized pepper confit, melt the butter in a heavy skillet. Add the peppers, onions, and garlic and sauté for 3 minutes, or until they are soft.

Add the thyme, sugar, salt, and pepper and cook over low heat for 20 to 30 minutes, stirring occasionally.

Add the wine and vinegar, bring to a boil, decrease to medium heat, and cook for 15 to 20 minutes, or until the peppers are caramelized. Cool.

Assembly

Preheat the oven to 375°.

Spray 6 stack cylinders with vegetable spray and place them on a sheet pan.

Layer the stacks in the following order: 1 polenta round, $1/4$ cup pepper confit, 2 tablespoons feta. Repeat, ending with feta. Press down gently but firmly. The stacks can be made ahead to this point and chilled.

Place the sheet pans with the stacks in the preheated oven and bake for 10 minutes.

To serve, slide a spatula under each stack and transfer to a serving plate. Unmold, garnish with chopped chives and Parmesan, and serve.

Shortcut Stacks

Purchase ready-made polenta rolls and cut them into rounds. Of course, homemade or 5-minute polenta is always better.

Herbed Mushroom Stacks with Vanilla-Balsamic Glaze

These wild mushroom pancakes are just delicious. Try them as a side dish with a roast or made larger and stacked as an entrée. The possibilities are endless. These are "free-form" stacks, requiring no cylinder—however, if your pancakes turn out irregular, you can trim them to 3 inches and use a cylinder to stack them.

Planning Ahead

- Prepare the mushroom pancakes early in the day and chill, covered.

- The day before or early in the day, cook the corn kernels and chill.

- Prepare the glaze the day before, cover, and chill.

2 ears fresh corn

MUSHROOM PANCAKES

1 cup cleaned, stemmed, and chopped portobello mushrooms

1 cup shiitake mushrooms, cleaned and stemmed

1 cup brown mushrooms, cleaned and stemmed

2 tablespoons butter

3 cloves garlic, peeled and minced

2 eggs

1 cup all-purpose flour

$1^1/_2$ cups milk

1 teaspoon paprika

$^1/_2$ teaspoon Colman's mustard powder

3 tablespoons chopped fresh basil

1 tablespoon chopped fresh thyme

$^1/_4$ cup chopped sundried tomatoes

$^1/_2$ teaspoon baking powder

$^1/_4$ teaspoon baking soda

$^1/_2$ teaspoon salt

Freshly ground black pepper to taste

$^1/_4$ cup minced chives

$^1/_2$ cup clarified butter (page 161)

1 cup boursin-pepper cheese, room temperature

$3^1/_2$ to 4 cups packed mesclun

$1^3/_4$ cups Vanilla-Balsamic Glaze (recipe follows)

Advance Preparation

Cut off the corn kernels and cook them in boiling salted water for 3 minutes. Drain and set aside.

To make the herbed mushroom pancakes, finely mince together all the mushrooms in a food processor using on-off pulses.

In a large skillet, sauté the mushrooms in the butter, until they start giving up liquid. Add the garlic and continue to cook until almost dry. Cool slightly.

Whisk together the eggs, flour, milk, paprika, mustard, basil, thyme, tomatoes, baking powder, soda, salt, pepper, and chives. Add the mushrooms and mix well. The batter should have the consistency of medium-thick pancake batter.

Heat a small nonstick skillet and brush with the clarified butter. Pour 2 tablespoons (about 1 ounce) batter into the skillet and spread to make a 3-inch round. Cook until the edges become dry and bubbles form on top. Turn the pancake over and cook until golden brown. Place the pancakes on a sheet pan lined with parchment. You will need 24 pancakes.

Assembly

"Frost" one side of each pancake with $2^1/_2$ teaspoons of boursin cheese. Layer the stacks in the following order: 1 pancake, cheese, 2 teaspoons corn, $^1/_4$ cup mesclun, a drizzle of balsamic glaze. Repeat, then top the stack with a third pancake. You will have 4 pancakes per serving.

To serve, slide a spatula under each stack and transfer to a serving plate. Surround it with a drizzle of glaze and serve.

VANILLA-BALSAMIC GLAZE
YIELD: $1^3/_4$ CUPS

$1^1/_2$ cups sugar

$1^1/_2$ cups water

$^1/_4$ teaspoon vanilla

$^1/_2$ cup balsamic vinegar

Boil together the sugar and water for 10 minutes, or until syrupy. Add the vanilla and vinegar. Boil until thickened, about 10 minutes. Be careful not to burn the sauce. Serve warm. Keep up to 2 weeks in the refrigerator. Reheat to use.

Grilled Vegetable and Parmesan Polenta Stacks

YIELD: 6 SERVINGS

I first created these stacks for my friends Marie and Jo Scarpa. Joe is a vegetarian, and this was a potluck dinner at their home. He loved it.

Planning Ahead

- Prepare the red pepper confit early in the day or the day before and refrigerate it, covered. Warm it before using.

- Grill the vegetables early in the day.

POLENTA

1 (13$^1/_2$-ounce) package 5-minute polenta (page 164)

$^1/_2$ cup grated Parmesan cheese

VEGETABLES

3 zucchini, cut lengthwise into $^1/_4$-inch slices

3 ears corn

1 large eggplant, cut into $^1/_4$-inch slices

3 large portobello mushrooms, cleaned and stemmed

Extra virgin olive oil

1$^1/_2$ cups grated Parmesan cheese

3 large tomatoes, cut into $^1/_4$-inch slices

1 (12-ounce) jar artichoke hearts, drained and chopped

1$^1/_2$ cups Caramelized Red Pepper and Onion Confit (recipe follows)

Advance Preparation

To make the polenta, prepare the polenta according to the recipe on page 164, adding $^1/_2$ cup grated Parmesan cheese and mixing well. Pour the hot polenta into a lightly greased half sheet pan (12 by 17 inches) and smooth evenly. Let rest 20 minutes to firm up. (You can speed this up by chilling the tray of polenta.) With a 3-inch-diameter stack cylinder or soup can, cut out 18 polenta rounds. Set aside. Freeze any leftover polenta for another use or future stacks.

To make the vegetables, grill, roast, or broil the zucchini, the corn, the eggplant, and the mushrooms. To grill, brush both sides of each vegetable lightly with the olive oil. Place on a medium-hot grill and cook until lightly browned, 5 to 7 minutes. Turn and brown the other side. Set aside.

Chop the grilled zucchini, cut the corn from the cob, and mix them together. Set aside. Chop the portobello mushrooms. You should have about $^3/_4$ cup. Set aside.

Assembly

Preheat the oven to 350°.

Spray 6 stack cylinders with vegetable spray and place them on a sheet pan. Layer the stacks in the following order: 1 polenta round, 1 slice of eggplant (you may have to cut the eggplant slice to fit; one easy way is to make a cut from the center to one edge and then slide the slice over itself, forming a smaller circle), 1 tablespoon cheese, 1 tomato slice, 1 tablespoon mushrooms, 2 tablespoons zucchini and corn, 1 tablespoon artichoke hearts, 1 polenta round, and 2 tablespoons red pepper confit. Then, repeat the layers, ending the second layer with the artichoke hearts. Press down gently but firmly. Garnish with a leftover piece of polenta cut into a decorative shape. Sprinkle the top with 1 tablespoon grated cheese.

The stacks can be chilled at this point and reheated later or baked now at 350° for 10 minutes. Remove the stacks from the oven, let rest 5 minutes, unmold, and serve.

CARAMELIZED RED PEPPER AND ONION CONFIT
YIELD: ABOUT 2 CUPS

$4^1/_2$ ounces sweet butter

3 large onions, peeled, halved and thinly sliced

4 cloves garlic, minced

1 pound red bell peppers, seeded and thinly sliced

1 tablespoon fresh thyme, minced

4 tablespoons brown sugar

Salt and freshly ground black pepper to taste

1 cup dry white wine

$^1/_3$ cup balsamic vinegar

In a large, heavy skillet, melt the butter. Add the onions, garlic, and peppers and sauté for 5 minutes, or until the onions are soft and beginning to brown. Add the thyme, sugar, salt, and pepper and cook over low heat for 30 to 45 minutes, or until the vegetables are very soft. Add the wine and vinegar and increase the heat to a boil. Decrease the heat and allow the confit to simmer gently, stirring occasionally, until the mixture is caramelized and thick, about 20 minutes. Remove from the heat and let cool. The mixture should not be runny. If so, simmer 10 minutes longer or until the liquid is evaporated.

Note: This confit is also terrific with omelets, bruschetta, wrapped in phyllo and baked, or simply with crackers and goat cheese for an appetizer.

Roasted Vine Tomatoes, Pesto, Mozzarella di Bufala, and Pine Nuts with Sundried Tomato Vinaigrette

YIELD: 6 SERVINGS

The essence of pure summer—basil and tomatoes—one of my favorite flavor combinations. This is salad-like in taste and texture and can be served as a first course salad.

Planning Ahead

- Prepare the roasted tomatoes the day before.
- Prepare the pesto the day before and chill, covered with plastic wrap.
- Prepare the vinaigrette the day before and chill.
- Assemble the stacks 2 hours prior to serving and chill.

TIP: Unwrap and drain the mozzarella. Place the round of cheese on a flat surface and cut straight down into slices using a taut piece (about 10 inches) of dental floss.

8 tomatoes, 3 inches in diameter, sliced into 24 equal rounds, discarding the end pieces

Salt and freshly ground black pepper to taste

$1/4$ cup extra virgin olive oil

24 fresh basil leaves

12 slices mozzarella di bufala, $1/4$ inch thick

$1/2$ cup toasted pine nuts (page 161)

$3/4$ cup pesto (page 160)

1 cup Sundried Tomato Vinaigrette (recipe follows)

1 tomato, seeded and diced, for garnish

Advance Preparation

Preheat the oven to 250°.

Spread 18 of the tomato slices in 1 layer on a parchment-lined baking sheet. Reserve the remaining tomato slices for the stack base. Sprinkle the slices with salt and pepper and drizzle lightly with olive oil. Bake for 2 to 3 hours, or until the slices are slightly dried but still moist. Cool.

Assembly

Spray 6 stack cylinders with vegetable spray and place them on a sheet pan. Layer the stacks in the following order: 1 fresh tomato slice, 2 basil leaves, 1 slice mozzarella, 2 teaspoons pine nuts, 1 tablespoon pesto, 1 roasted tomato slice. Repeat the layers beginning with the basil and ending with the third roasted tomato slice. Press down gently but firmly and refrigerate until serving time.

To serve cold, slide a spatula under each stack cylinder and transfer to a serving plate, unmold, garnish with the additional basil and pine nuts, and spoon vinaigrette around the base. Spoon tiny dots of additional pesto around the edge of the plate and serve.

To serve warm, place the stacks in a preheated oven set at 350° for 10 minutes, or until heated through. Slide a spatula under each stack cylinder and transfer to a serving plate. Unmold, garnish with diced tomatoes, spoon vinaigrette and additional pesto around the base, and serve.

SUNDRIED TOMATO VINAIGRETTE

YIELD: ABOUT 1 CUP

2 tablespoons Dijon mustard

$1/_3$ cup red wine vinegar

1 clove garlic, minced

$2/_3$ cup extra virgin olive oil

3 tablespoons chopped parsley

$1/_4$ cup drained and diced oil-packed
    sundried tomatoes

Salt and freshly ground black pepper
    to taste

To make the vinaigrette, place the mustard, vinegar, and garlic in a bowl and whisk until blended. Slowly add the olive oil, whisking until blended and thickened. Stir in the parsley, sundried tomatoes, salt, and pepper. The vinaigrette will keep, covered, in the refrigerator for about 4 days.

Shortcut Stacks

- Purchase a quality pesto.
- Purchase a tomato vinaigrette.
- Use drained oil-packed sundried tomatoes in place of the roasted tomatoes.

Eggplant-Tomato Stacks

YIELD: 6 SERVINGS

With eggplant, peppers, and tomatoes, this is an elegant way to begin any dinner party, and a perfect summer stack. These stacks can also be served warm, if desired.

Planning Ahead

- Prepare and stack early in the day and chill.

- Prepare the vinaigrette the day before, cover, and chill.

$1/_2$ cup extra virgin olive oil

1 to 2 teaspoons cumin

$1/_2$ teaspoon salt

$1/_8$ teaspoon freshly ground black pepper

1 large eggplant, thinly sliced (about $1/_4$ inch thick)

2 red bell peppers, quartered and seeded

2 yellow bell peppers, quartered and seeded

5 tomatoes, sliced into 18 $1/_4$-inch-thick slices

1 cup goat cheese, boursin, or feta cheese

$1/_2$ cup chopped cilantro

$1/_4$ cup chopped chives

$2/_3$ cup Garlic Vinaigrette (recipe follows)

Advance Preparation

Mix together the olive oil, cumin, salt, and pepper and lightly brush the mixture on the eggplant slices. Grill the slices over medium-hot coals until golden brown and soft. (Or grill on the stovetop using a grill pan.) Set aside.

Char the red and yellow peppers on the grill, under the broiler, or over a hot flame. Then roll the peppers in paper towels and place them in a plastic bag for 10 minutes to steam. Remove the peppers and, with a sharp knife, scrape the blackened skin off and discard the skin. Julienne the peppers. Mix the peppers together and set aside.

Assembly

Spray 6 stack cylinders with vegetable spray and place them on a sheet pan.

Layer the stacks in the following order: 1 tomato slice, 1 eggplant slice, 1 tablespoon goat cheese, 2 tablespoons peppers. Repeat the layers and top the stack with a third tomato slice. Press down firmly but gently to compact layers. Chill until serving time

To serve, slide a spatula under each stack cylinder and transfer to a serving plate. Carefully unmold. Garnish with a scatter of cilantro and chives around the stacks. Crumble any leftover goat cheese on top, spoon vinaigrette over and around the stacks, and serve.

GARLIC VINAIGRETTE

YIELD: $^3/_4$ CUP

3 cloves garlic, minced

$^1/_2$ teaspoon salt

$^1/_4$ teaspoon freshly ground black pepper

1 tablespoon Dijon mustard

3 tablespoons red wine vinegar

$^1/_2$ cup extra virgin olive oil

1 tablespoon chopped chives

1 tablespoon chopped parsley

Place garlic, salt, pepper, mustard, and vinegar in a bowl and whisk together. Slowly add the oil, whisking, until the dressing thickens. Stir in the chives and parsley.

Smoked Salmon with Dilled Potato Waffles

YIELD: 6 SERVINGS

I created this recipe when I was trying to come up with a new way to serve smoked salmon. Somehow waffles came to mind, and I began to experiment with different flavors. Use your imagination. Try tarragon waffles, sundried tomato waffles, corn waffles—you choose. Use a heart-shaped waffle iron for Valentine's Day. I have also made these as free-form stacks—no cylinders, just small, uniform waffles. Also try dilled pancakes or blini.

Planning Ahead

- Have all the ingredients ready to stack.
- Prepare the waffle batter early in the day and chill, covered.
- Bake the waffles just prior to serving and stacking—you will need 18 3-inch rounds or 18 sections from 5 whole waffles.
- Prepare the dressing the day before, cover, and chill.

DILLED POTATO WAFFLES

4 cups mashed potatoes (page 163)

$1/_2$ cup presifted all-purpose flour

3 eggs

2 tablespoons chopped fresh dill

1 teaspoon baking powder

2 cups (about 16 ounces) smoked salmon, or $2^1/_2$ cups grilled salmon, flaked

$3/_4$ cup Sour Cream–Dill Dressing (recipe follows)

$1^1/_2$ cups minced whole green onions

6 teaspoons (about 1 ounce) caviar (optional)

Advance Preparation

To make the dilled potato waffles, combine all of the waffle ingredients. It should be the consistency of very thick pancake batter. Preheat a waffle iron and brush the surface with melted butter. Prepare the waffles according to the machine instructions and cook until the waffles are golden and crisp. Trim to 3 inches in diameter. Repeat with remaining batter. Keep the prepared waffles warm in a 250° oven.

Note: If you are making free-form stacks, do not trim the waffles. Most waffle irons are divided into four small sections. Use one section for each layer. Each stack will have 3 layers (or sections). Layer, garnish, and serve immediately.

Assembly

Spray the inside of a stack cylinder with vegetable spray and place on a small serving platter. Place a waffle round in the bottom of a cylinder and layer with 1 tablespoon dressing, followed by 1 tablespoon green onions and $1^{1}/_{2}$ ounces salmon. Repeat twice for each stack, using three waffles per stack. Press down on the stack gently but firmly and remove the cylinder. Garnish with a dollop of dressing and a teaspoon of caviar. Sprinkle minced green onions around base of stack and serve.

SOUR CREAM–DILL DRESSING

YIELD: ABOUT 2 CUPS

1 cup sour cream

$^{1}/_{2}$ cup mayonnaise

2 tablespoons chopped fresh dill

2 teaspoons grated onion

1 teaspoon grated lemon zest

2 hard-boiled eggs, peeled and chopped

2 teaspoons minced fresh parsley

Salt and freshly ground black pepper to taste

1 teaspoon freshly squeezed lemon juice

Combine all of the ingredients and mix well. Chill until serving time.

This dressing is also wonderful with poached salmon, grilled scallops, or shrimp.

Fruited Saint André Stacks

YIELD: 20 TO 30 SERVINGS

This is one of my all-time favorite party presentations. It feeds a lot of people, looks stunning, and tastes divine. It can be made with smaller, 3-inch individual Saint André cheeses for intimate gatherings. Do not buy Saint André cheese if it is overripe or smells slightly of vinegar or ammonia. Make sure the cheese has never been frozen. If it has an uneven texture, a cracked or dry rind, or if the inside is not creamy, it may have been frozen.

Planning Ahead
Prepare the stack and wrap it in plastic wrap 2 hours before serving.

1 whole Saint André cheese, chilled

1¹/₂ cups each of three fruits from this list: strawberries, raspberries, blueberries, sliced kiwi, sliced peaches, sliced mangoes, plums, pitted cherries, apricots

Toasted baguette slices or crackers

Assembly
Using dental floss (see Tip), cut the chilled Saint André cheese into 4 equal layers. Place the bottom layer on a serving tray and cover it evenly with 1¹/₂ cups of fruit.

Top with the second layer, another 1¹/₂ cups of fruit, then the third layer and 1¹/₂ cups of fruit.

Place the top of the cheese over the last layer of fruit and press down firmly. Wrap securely in plastic wrap and chill for 2 hours.

To serve, unwrap the cheese and allow it to warm to room temperature. Garnish decoratively with an additional combination of fruit. Serve surrounded with bread slices or a variety of cheese crackers.

Note: This is also a lovely summer dessert when drizzled with a fruited honey and served with cinnamon bruschetta or shortbread cookies.

TIP: To cut even layers of the cheese, wrap a piece of dental floss around the circumference at the point you want the cheese cut. Cross the two ends of the floss in front of you, keeping it lined up straight around the cheese. Pull the ends straight out to the side until the cheese layer is cut all the way through. This is also a great way to cut cake layers.

Antipasto and Polenta with Balsamic and Sundried Tomato Vinaigrette

YIELD: 6 SERVINGS

This could double as a first course, salad stack, or could be made in small, 1^1/$_2$-inch ring cylinders and served as hors d'oeuvres with drinks. The stacks in the photo opposite were made with a triangle mold. Whichever way they're served, they're good.

Planning Ahead

- Prepare the polenta rounds the day before and chill. Bring to room temperature before stacking.

- Prep all of the vegetables and sauté the pancetta early in the day.

- Make the vinaigrette the day before and chill.

TIP: For fast bacon or pancetta bits, slice the entire pound of partially frozen bacon diagonally into ^{1}/$_4$-inch slices. Fry the desired portion, breaking it up as it cooks. Freeze any raw bacon for later use.

1 (13^1/$_2$-ounce) package 5-minute polenta (page 164)

2 tablespoons butter, room temperature

^{1}/$_2$ cup freshly grated Parmesan cheese

^{1}/$_2$ cup drained and finely minced oil-packed sundried tomatoes

Salt and freshly ground pepper to taste

12 pieces pancetta, diced

18 fresh asparagus spears

3 red bell peppers, seeded, charred or roasted, peeled, and sliced thinly

1 yellow bell pepper, seeded, charred or roasted, peeled, and sliced thinly

1 zucchini, sliced, grilled, and chopped

12 marinated artichoke hearts, drained and quartered

Fresh basil, for garnish

Advance Preparation

Prepare polenta according to package directions. Add butter, Parmesan, and sundried tomatoes and season with salt and pepper. Pour into an 12 by 17-inch half sheet pan and smooth. Allow to set 15 to 20 minutes. Polenta should be ^{1}/$_3$ to ^{1}/$_4$ inch thick.

Sauté the pancetta until crisp, about 10 minutes, and drain. Set aside.

To cook the asparagus spears, trim off the tough ends. Place the spears in a large skillet with 2 inches of boiling water, cover, and cook for 3 minutes. Drain and coarsely chop.

Cut the polenta into 3-inch rounds, about ^{1}/$_4$ inch thick. You will need 1^1/$_4$-inch-thick rounds.

Assembly

Preheat the oven to 350°.

Spray 6 stack cylinders with vegetable spray and place them on a sheet pan. Layer the ingredients in the following order: 1 round polenta, 1 tablespoon asparagus, 2 tablespoons red and yellow peppers, 1 tablespoon pancetta, 1 tablespoon zucchini, 4 pieces artichoke hearts. Repeat the layers once more, ending with the third slice of polenta. Press the layers down tightly and bake for 10 minutes.

To serve, slide a spatula under each stack cylinder and transfer to a serving plate. Unmold and top with 2 tablespoons pancetta and a sprinkle of basil. Spoon vinaigrette around the stack and serve.

BALSAMIC AND SUNDRIED TOMATO VINAIGRETTE
YIELD: ABOUT 1 CUP

2 cloves garlic, minced

2 tablespoons Dijon mustard

3 tablespoons drained and diced oil-packed sundried tomatoes

4$^1/_2$ tablespoons balsamic vinegar

$^2/_3$ cup extra virgin olive oil

Salt and freshly ground black pepper to taste

2 tablespoons chopped fresh parsley

Note: To achieve a stack like the one in the photograph, use a triangular stacking mold.

Place the garlic, mustard, and sundried tomatoes in a small mixing bowl. Add the vinegar and whisk until blended. Slowly add the olive oil in a thin stream while whisking to emulsify. Whisk in the salt, pepper, and parsley. Cover and chill until needed.

Shortcut Stacks

- Purchase ready-made polenta and cut into rounds.
- Purchase a fine-quality balsamic or sundried tomato dressing.

Curried Walnut and Blue Cheese Stacks

YIELD: 10 TO 12 SERVINGS

A fabulous holiday appetizer—easy to do ahead and beautiful. The combination of blue cheese and cranberries is unexpected and delicious. Try making this as small $1^1/_2$-inch stacks for individual appetizers at a sit-down holiday dinner.

Planning Ahead

- Prepare the stack the day before, cover, and chill. Unmold just before serving.

- Prepare the cranberries the day before.

2 cups crumbled Maytag blue cheese

Scant $1/_2$ cup goat cheese

Scant $1/_2$ cup cream cheese

$1/_4$ cup butter, room temperature

$1/_2$ cup chopped chives

2 tablespoons port

3 tablespoons chopped fresh parsley

1 tablespoon chopped fresh thyme

1 tablespoon chopped fresh sage

1 (16-ounce) package fresh cranberries, washed and picked over

1 cup sugar

2 cups water

1 tablespoon grated lemon zest

$1/_4$ cup dried cranberries

1 cup Toasted Curried Mixed Nuts (recipe follows)

Advance Preparation

In a food processor, combine $1^1/_2$ cups of blue cheese, the goat cheese, the cream cheese, and the butter. Process until smooth. Pulse in the chives and port. Set aside.

Mix together the parsley, thyme, and sage in another bowl.

Combine the cranberries, sugar, water, and lemon zest in a medium saucepan. Bring to a boil over medium-high heat. Reduce heat to low and simmer until thickened. Cool and chill.

Assembly

Spray a large decorative metal mold, pyramid-shaped mold, or 2 stack cylinders with vegetable spray and line with plastic wrap, allowing the plastic to extend over the edges. Layer in the following order: one third of the cheese mixture, 2 tablespoons dried cranberries, 3 tablespoons crumbled blue cheese, 1 tablespoon herbs, 3 tablespoons curried nuts. Repeat the layers, ending with the last third of the cheese mixture. Press down gently but firmly. Chill for at least 4 hours.

To serve, with a flat spatula transfer the mold or stacks to a serving platter, unmold, peel off the plastic wrap, and spoon the cranberry sauce around the base. Serve with toasted bread rounds, crackers, or toasted pita triangles.

Toasted Curried Mixed Nuts

YIELD: 6 SERVINGS

These are also wonderful in spinach salads with fresh pears and Gorgonzola cheese, or stuffed into apple cavities prior to baking.

1 teaspoon curry powder

$^3/_4$ teaspoon ground cumin

$^1/_2$ teaspoon ground ginger

$^1/_8$ teaspoon freshly ground nutmeg

$^1/_8$ teaspoon ground cinnamon

$^1/_8$ teaspoon cayenne

$^1/_2$ cup walnut pieces

1 cup pecan pieces

1 cup sliced almonds

2 tablespoons sweet butter

1 tablespoon freshly squeezed orange juice

$1^1/_2$ tablespoons brown sugar

$1^1/_2$ tablespoons sugar

$^1/_2$ teaspoon salt

Mix together the curry, cumin, ginger, nutmeg, cinnamon, and cayenne. Place nuts in a large skillet and cook over medium-high heat for 2 to 3 minutes. Stir in the butter and spices. Add the orange juice, sugars, and salt and cook, stirring constantly, for 6 to 7 minutes. See that the nuts do not burn. Spray a sheet pan with vegetable spray. Spread the nuts on the sheet pan to cool completely.

Note: These spicy nuts can be placed in a resealable bag and frozen.

Avocado, Tomato, and Phyllo Stacks

SALAD STACKS

Avocado, Tomato, and Phyllo Stacks

YIELD: 6 SERVINGS

This was my first free-form stack. Taking the premise of this recipe—phyllo squares stacked with fillings—you can create many impressive dishes. Refer to the Stacks Matrix for some flavor ideas. This particular recipe has a light Mexican flavor.

Planning Ahead

- The phyllo squares can be made early in the day and set aside at room temperature.

- All the ingredients for the filling can be prepared ahead of time, with the exception of the avocado. Mash the avocado at the last minute and mix it with the prepared ingredients.

- The garnish can be prepared and refrigerated, covered, 3 hours ahead.

- If you choose to make the phyllo "flowers," they, too, can be made early in the day.

TIP: When coating phyllo sheets with butter, pour melted butter into a small spray bottle and lightly spray the phyllo. This allows you to use only a little fat with the same results. To keep the butter liquid, place the spray bottle in a pan of very warm water.

PHYLLO SQUARES

12 sheets phyllo dough

6 tablespoons butter, melted

$^3/_4$ cup grated Parmesan cheese

SALAD FILLING

3 avocados, peeled, pitted, and diced

$1^1/_2$ tomatoes, diced

$^1/_2$ cup minced red bell pepper

$^1/_2$ cup minced green bell pepper

$^1/_2$ cup minced yellow bell pepper

$^1/_2$ cup chopped fresh cilantro

$^1/_4$ teaspoon cumin

2 teaspoons Cholulu hot sauce (or $^1/_2$ teaspoon Tabasco sauce)

1 tablespoon freshly squeezed lime juice

Salt and freshly ground black pepper to taste

$^1/_2$ cup sour cream

$^1/_2$ cup diced tomatoes, for garnish

$^1/_2$ cup chopped cilantro, for garnish

Advance Preparation

Preheat oven to 375°.

To make the phyllo squares, place a sheet of phyllo on a clean, dry surface. Brush or spray the square with melted butter and sprinkle with 1 tablespoon Parmesan cheese. Top with a second sheet, repeat. Top with the third and fourth sheets, repeating the steps. Fold in half and cut into 8 equal squares. Repeat with the remaining 8 sheets of phyllo, using 4 sheets at a time. Sprinkle all of the squares with any remaining Parmesan and bake for 5 to 7 minutes, or until golden. Cool. You will need 18 squares of phyllo.

To make the filling, coarsely mash the avocado and gently stir in the remaining ingredients. Set aside.

Assembly

Place a phyllo square on each of 6 serving plates. Frost with 1 tablespoon sour cream. Gently spread 2 tablespoons avocado mixture on top. Then top with another phyllo square, 1 tablespoon sour cream, and more avocado. Place the third phyllo square on top and garnish with a dollop of sour cream and a sprinkling of tomato and cilantro. Serve immediately.

Note: The top phyllo square can be more decorative if you make a "phyllo flower." After buttering a phyllo sheet, cut it into 3 by 3-inch squares and crunch each square to resemble a flower. Bake at 375° for 5 to 7 minutes, or until golden. For appetizer-sized stacks, cut the phyllo into 1$\frac{1}{2}$-inch squares.

Field Greens and Grilled Apple Stacks with Grilled Apple, Fig, and Balsamic Vinegar Dressing

I suggest using the wonderful fig balsamic available through Surfas Gourmet Foods and Sur la Table (see Resources, page 169). This stack is terrific as a light entrée when layered with diced grilled chicken or turkey. You can also substitute grilled pears, peaches, or nectarines. When using pears, try almonds instead of walnuts. For peaches, use macadamia nuts.

Planning Ahead

- Prepare the dressing the day before, cover, and chill.
- Grill the apple slices early in the day; cover.
- Toast the walnuts the day before.
- Assemble the salad 1 to 2 hours before serving and chill.

3 Golden Delicious apples, 3 inches in diameter, sliced $1/4$ inch thick (12 slices) and seeded

3 tablespoons butter, melted

3 tablespoons superfine sugar

12 slices herbed goat cheese, $1/4$ inch thick

$1/2$ cup toasted and chopped walnuts, (page 161)

3 cups mixed baby field greens or young mixed lettuces

$1 1/2$ cups Grilled Apple, Fig, and Balsamic Vinegar Dressing (recipe follows)

Advance Preparation

To prepare the apples, brush the apple slices with melted butter and dust one side with sugar. Grill the apples on both sides until golden and soft, about 5 minutes, or brown them under the broiler or on a stovetop grill.

Assembly

Spray 6 stack cylinders with vegetable spray and place them on a sheet pan. Layer in the following order: 1 grilled apple slice, 1 slice goat cheese crumbled in an even layer, $1/_2$ tablespoon walnuts, $1/_4$ cup field greens or baby lettuces. Repeat the layers, ending with the greens. Press down gently but firmly and chill until serving time, at least 1 hour.

To serve, slide a spatula under each stack cylinder and transfer to a serving plate. Unmold, spoon dressing around the base, drizzle a small amount of dressing over the top of the stack, and serve.

GRILLED APPLE, FIG, AND BALSAMIC VINEGAR DRESSING
YIELD: $1\,^1/_2$ CUPS

2 tablespoons honey mustard

1 apple, peeled, seeded, sliced, and grilled or baked until tender

$^1/_4$ cup fig-balsamic vinegar (see Note)

$^3/_4$ cup canola oil

1 tablespoon walnut oil

Place the mustard, grilled apple, and vinegar in a food processor and blend until smooth. Slowly add the oils and blend until thickened. Chill.

Note: If you cannot find fig balsamic (see Resources, page 169), use $^1/_4$ cup balsamic vinegar mixed with 1 tablespoon fig jam or fig honey.

Tomato-Couscous Stacks

YIELD: 6 SERVINGS

This delicious warm salad, served on cold greens, is also great for picnics, served at room temperature (after baking). Pack the cold greens and vinaigrette separately. It is also wonderful with the addition of grilled diced chicken or shrimp, making it an entrée.

Planning Ahead

- Prepare stacks ahead and chill. Bake just before serving.
- Prepare the greens, cheese, and balsamic vinaigrette early.

1$^1/_2$ cups couscous

4 tablespoons extra virgin olive oil

1 large eggplant, diced

4 cloves garlic, minced

1 large red bell pepper, diced

1 large yellow bell pepper, diced

$^1/_2$ cup diced whole green onions

Salt and freshly ground black pepper to taste

4 tablespoons chopped fresh basil

3$^1/_2$ cups fresh spinach, washed, torn into small bite-size pieces, and chilled

2$^1/_2$ cups watercress, chopped and chilled

6 tomatoes, 3 inches in diameter, each sliced into 3 even slices (discard the ends or save for another use)

$^2/_3$ cup freshly grated Parmesan cheese

$^1/_2$ cup minced chives

$^2/_3$ cup Balsamic Vinaigrette (recipe follows)

Advance Preparation

Prepare the couscous according to package instructions, adding 1 tablespoon olive oil to the water. Set aside.

In a large skillet, sauté the eggplant in 3 tablespoons olive oil until softened and browned. Add the garlic, peppers, and onions and continue to cook until the vegetables are tender, about 15 minutes. Season with salt and pepper, add the basil, and stir well to blend. Add the cooked couscous and stir well.

Assembly

Preheat the oven to 350°.

Spray 6 stack cylinders with vegetable spray and place them on a sheet pan. Mix together the spinach and watercress. Layer the stacks in the following order: 1 tomato slice, $1/4$ cup couscous, 1 tablespoon Parmesan, 2 tablespoons spinach-watercress. Repeat and top with a tomato slice and 2 tablespoons couscous. Press down gently but firmly. Sprinkle 1 tablespoon Parmesan over each stack. Bake at 350° for 10 minutes.

To serve, slide a spatula under each stack cylinder and transfer to a serving plate lined with the remaining spinach and watercress. Unmold the stacks and sprinkle with the remaining Parmesan and the chopped chives. Drizzle with vinaigrette.

Shortcut Stacks

- Use a packaged flavored couscous (the flavor won't be exactly the same, but it is faster).

- Purchase prepared greens.

- Have your Parmesan grated when you buy it. Most good supermarkets will provide this service.

- Purchase a quality balsamic salad dressing.

BALSAMIC VINAIGRETTE
YIELD: 6 SERVINGS

1 tablespoon Dijon mustard

4 tablespoons balsamic vinegar

1 clove garlic, minced

$1/2$ cup extra virgin olive oil

Salt and freshly ground black pepper to taste

1 tablespoon minced fresh parsley

Whisk together the mustard, the vinegar, and the garlic. Slowly add the oil, whisking to emulsify and blend well. Add the salt, pepper, and the parsley, and blend.

Tex-Mex Tomato Stacks

YIELD: 6 SERVINGS

When I had my restaurant, Panache, we served this salad from our gourmet-to-go as well as on the menu. The customers couldn't get enough of it. It is the perfect stack for summer when tomatoes are at their peak. Great with grilled chicken, beef, or fish.

Planning Ahead

- This stack can be made 2 hours ahead and chilled. Garnish just before serving.

- Make the tomatoes early in the day to allow flavors to blend. (If you are unable to locate yellow tomatoes, use all red tomatoes.)

TIP: When making guacamole or dicing avocados, try cutting the avocado in half, removing the pit, and forcing it, meat side down, through a wire cooking rack set over a bowl. It works great.

1 cup vegetable oil

$1/_2$ cup white wine vinegar

3 tablespoons sugar

3 cloves garlic

8 ounces green chile salsa

2 teaspoons minced fresh oregano, or
  1 teaspoon dried

$1/_4$ teaspoon celery seed

$1/_4$ teaspoon cumin

Salt and freshly ground black pepper
  to taste

6 whole green onions, diced

1 cup diced celery

5 red tomatoes, seeded and chopped

5 yellow tomatoes, seeded and chopped

4 anchovy fillets, minced

$3/_4$ cup minced fresh parsley

4 ounces green chiles, diced (about
  $1/_2$ cup)

6 slices mozzarella

1 avocado, peeled, pitted, and diced

6 red lettuce leaves, rinsed and trimmed

$1/_4$ cup chopped fresh parsley, for garnish

6 slices avocado, for garnish

$1/_2$ cup diced tomatoes, for garnish

Place the oil, vinegar, sugar, garlic, salsa, oregano, celery seed, cumin, salt, and pepper in a food processor and blend for 5 to 10 seconds, until mixed together but not smooth. Pour into a glass bowl. Add the green onions, celery, tomatoes, anchovies, $1/_2$ cup parsley, and green chiles. Chill for several hours.

Assembly

Spray 6 stack cylinders with vegetable spray and place them on a sheet pan lined with parchment. Drain the tomato mixture and reserve the juice. Layer the stacks in the following order: $1/4$ cup drained tomato mixture, 1 slice mozzarella, $1 1/2$ tablespoons avocado, $1/4$ cup drained tomato mixture. Press down on each stack firmly but gently. Refrigerate until serving time.

To serve, line 6 serving plates with lettuce leaves. Slide a spatula under each stack cylinder and transfer to a serving plate. Unmold and garnish with a sprinkling of parsley, avocado slices, or diced tomato. Spoon a little reserved marinade as dressing over the lettuce and serve.

Note: This is also good served with guacamole and sour cream.

Endive and Asian Pear Stacks

YIELD: 6 SERVINGS

If you want to turn a meal into something special, start it off with this salad. The pesto is also wonderful over pasta for a quick dinner. Create an entrée stack by adding skewered grilled shrimp.

Planning Ahead

- Make this salad, stack, and chill several hours ahead.
- Make the pesto the day before, cover, and chill.
- Make the balsamic dressing the day before, cover, and chill.

2 Asian pears, sliced $^1/_4$ inch thick and seeded (12 slices)

2 cups coarsely chopped radicchio

1 cup (8 ounces) Cambozola or other mild blue cheese, crumbled

$^3/_4$ cup Walnut Pesto (recipe follows)

2 cups coarsely chopped Belgian endive

$^3/_4$ cup Balsamic Vinaigrette (page 158)

Assembly

Spray 6 stack cylinders with vegetable spray and place them on a sheet pan. Layer in the following order: 1 slice Asian pear, $^1/_3$ cup radicchio, 1 tablespoon Cambozola, 1 tablespoon pesto, $^1/_3$ cup endive, 1 slice Asian pear, 1 tablespoon Cambozola, 1 tablespoon pesto. Press down gently but firmly and chill for 1 to 2 hours.

To serve, slide a spatula under each stack cylinder and transfer to a serving plate. Unmold, drizzle with 2 tablespoons balsamic vinaigrette, and serve.

WALNUT PESTO
YIELD: ABOUT 1$^1/_2$ CUPS

1 cup packed fresh basil leaves

1 cup packed fresh cilantro

$^1/_4$ cup packed fresh tarragon

$^1/_2$ cup chopped parsley

1 cup toasted walnuts (page 161)

$^1/_3$ cup balsamic vinegar

$^2/_3$ cup extra virgin olive oil

2 tablespoons walnut oil

Combine the basil, cilantro, tarragon, parsley, walnuts, and vinegar in a food processor and blend well. Slowly add the oils until the pesto is well mixed. The pesto should be fairly thick, not runny.

Note: This pesto is also terrific over linguine, with lots of fresh Parmesan cheese.

Shortcut Stacks
Buy a quality balsamic vinaigrette.

Tomato–Blue Cheese Stacks

This beautiful presentation marries two classic flavors—tomatoes and blue cheese. The cucumber adds color and crunch; the dressing is rich enough to complement the cheese. A terrific entertaining stack.

Planning Ahead

- Prepare and stack the salads several hours ahead.
- Make the vinaigrette the day before, cover, and chill.

6 tomatoes, 3 inches in diameter, each sliced into 3 even slices (discard the ends or use in soup)

$3/4$ cup crumbled Saint Agur or other quality blue cheese (Maytag, Roquefort, Cambozola)

3 cups mesclun

1 English cucumber, sliced very thin

$1/2$ cup Sundried Tomato–Balsamic Vinaigrette (recipe follows)

1 tomato, diced, for garnish

Assembly

Spray 6 stack cylinders with vegetable spray and place on a parchment- or wax paper–lined sheet pan. Layer the stacks in the following order: 1 tomato slice, 1 tablespoon blue cheese, $1/4$ cup of the mesclun, 1 layer cucumber slices. Repeat and top with a tomato slice. Press down gently but firmly and chill for at least 30 minutes and up to 4 hours.

To serve, slide a spatula under each stack cylinder and transfer to a serving plate. Unmold and drizzle with balsamic dressing. Garnish with the remaining sliced cucumbers and diced tomatoes.

Sundried Tomato–Balsamic Vinaigrette

YIELD: ABOUT $1/2$ CUP

1 clove garlic, minced

1 shallot, minced

1 tablespoon drained and minced oil-packed sundried tomatoes

1 tablespoon Dijon mustard

1 tablespoon chopped fresh basil

3 tablespoons balsamic vinegar

Salt and freshly ground black pepper to taste

$1/3$ cup extra virgin olive oil

1 tablespoon chopped fresh parsley

Whisk together the garlic, shallot, sundried tomatoes, mustard, basil, vinegar, salt, and pepper. Slowly add the oil, while whisking, until the vinaigrette is blended and thickened. Stir in the parsley.

Radicchio-Nectarine Summer Stacks

YIELD: 6 SERVINGS

Not only are the colors in this salad magnificent, the taste is divine. The combination of the crispy radicchio, the luscious fruit, and the blue cheese is, to my mind, just about perfect. Toasted walnuts add a little crunch.

Planning Ahead

- This whole stack can be made 2 hours ahead, making it a great choice for entertaining.
- The vinaigrette can be made the day before, covered, and refrigerated.

TIP: Toast large quantities of nuts ahead of time and store in the freezer. You will always have toasted nuts on hand.

1 1/2 large heads radicchio, chopped

6 ounces quality blue cheese (Saint Agur, Maytag, or Gorgonzola), crumbled

6 nectarines, coarsely chopped (if you have trouble finding nectarines, use peaches)

1/3 cup toasted walnuts, chopped (page 161)

Nectarine Vinaigrette (recipe follows)

Assembly

Spray 6 stack cylinders with vegetable spray and place them on a sheet pan. Layer stacks in the following order: 1/4 cup radicchio, 1 1/2 tablespoons blue cheese, 1/4 cup nectarine, 1 teaspoon walnuts. Repeat the layers. Press down gently but firmly. Refrigerate until serving time, chilling at least 1 hour.

To serve, slide a spatula under each stack cylinder and transfer to a serving plate. Spoon 2 tablespoons of dressing on the plate. Just prior to unmolding the salad, drizzle a little dressing over the salad, and serve.

NECTARINE VINAIGRETTE
YIELD: 2 CUPS

1 ripe nectarine, seeded and chopped

1 cup nectarine nectar (or peach nectar if nectarine nectar is unavailable)

1/4 cup Japanese seasoned rice wine vinegar

1 tablespoon sweet mustard

1 teaspoon sesame oil

2 tablespoons peanut oil or vegetable oil

Place all ingredients in a food processor and blend until smooth. Strain through a strainer and refrigerate.

Shortcut Stacks

Try substituting Consorzio's Passion Fruit or Mango Vinaigrette for the Nectarine Vinaigrette (see Resources, page 169).

Panzanella Stacks

YIELD: 6 SERVINGS

Italian bread salads have always been a favorite of mine, so it seemed natural to create a panzanella stack. They are also perfect picnic fare.

Planning Ahead
Prepare the stacks several hours ahead.

TIP: To moisten bread evenly without soaking, put water in a spray bottle and lightly spritz the bread.

PANZANELLA

6 slices 2-day-old coarse-textured bread such as country Italian, sheepherder's, or a heavy French bread

3 tomatoes, coarsely chopped

$1/2$ English cucumber, coarsely chopped

1 sweet Maui, Vidalia, or red onion, chopped

$1/2$ cup chopped fresh parsley

$1/4$ cup chopped fresh basil

Salt and freshly ground black pepper to taste

$1/4$ cup red wine vinegar

$1/2$ to $3/4$ cup extra virgin olive oil

3 tomatoes, 3 inches in diameter (or trim tomatoes to 3 inches), each sliced into 4 even slices

2 red bell peppers, charred, peeled, and julienned (see Tip, page 51)

1 (8-ounce) jar artichoke hearts, drained and chopped

6 sprigs fresh parsley, for garnish

3 tablespoons oil-packed sundried tomatoes, drained, for garnish

12 fresh basil leaves, for garnish

Advance Preparation

To make the panzanella, tear the bread into bite-size pieces, place it in a large bowl, and sprinkle it with just enough water to barely moisten the bread. Add the chopped tomatoes, cucumber, onion, parsley, basil, salt, and pepper. Toss. Whisk together the vinegar and oil. Pour the dressing, 1 table-spoon at a time, over the salad, tossing after each addition until the bread is moist but not soggy. Save any remaining dressing for another use.

Assembly

Spray 6 stack cylinders with vegetable spray and place them on a sheet pan. Place a tomato slice in the bottom of each cylinder. Then layer in the following order: $1/4$ cup panzanella, 1 tablespoon peppers, 1 tablespoon artichoke hearts, 1 tomato slice. Repeat the layers, ending with artichoke hearts. Press down gently but firmly. Chill stacks for an hour (or longer).

To serve, slide a spatula under each stack cylinder and transfer to a serving plate. Unmold, garnish with the parsley, sundried tomatoes, and basil leaves, and serve.

TIP: To char peppers, cut the peppers into quarters and seed. Brush the quarters with olive oil and place them skin side down, facing the heat, over hot coals, on a hot grill, or under the broiler, and cook until the skin chars, 4 to 5 minutes. Wrap the peppers in a paper towel and place them in a plastic bag for 5 to 10 minutes. (This steams the hot peppers.) Remove. With a sharp knife, scrape the charred skin off the pepper. Then julienne the peppers and proceed with the recipe.

Charred peppers can be made ahead, covered, and chilled. These peppers are also great if you purée them in a food processor, mix them with a little cream, and serve over pasta or as a sauce to grilled chicken.

Radicchio with Gorgonzola and Grilled Pears

Radicchio is such a wonderful lettuce. Not only is it a beautiful color, but it holds up very well to dressings without becoming instantly wilted. It also marries well with many other flavors, such as bacon, Parmesan, lemon, garlic, and anchovies.

Planning Ahead

- Prepare the stacks 2 to 3 hours in advance and chill.
- Prepare the vinaigrette the day before.
- Prepare the candied pecans several days in advance and store them in an airtight container.

3 pears

2 tablespoons melted butter

1$^1/_2$ cups coarsely chopped radicchio

$^3/_4$ cup coarsely chopped arugula

4 ounces goat cheese, sliced $^1/_4$ inch thick

$^1/_2$ cup plus 2 tablespoons crumbled Gorgonzola cheese

$^1/_2$ cup Candied Pecans (recipe follows), chopped

Pear-Honey Vinaigrette (recipe follows)

Advance Preparation

Slice the pears horizontally, into 12 rounds, remove seeds, and brush lightly with melted butter. Grill or broil the pears until just cooked but not mushy, 3 to 4 minutes. Set aside.

Chop the radicchio and arugula separately and set aside.

Have ready the crumbled Gorgonzola, the pecans, and the Pear-Honey Vinaigrette.

Assembly

Spray 6 stack cylinders with vegetable spray and place them on a sheet pan. Layer as follows: 1 grilled pear slice, 2 teaspoons pecans, 1$^1/_2$ slices goat cheese, $^1/_4$ cup radicchio, 1 grilled pear slice, 2 teaspoons pecans, 1 tablespoon Gorgonzola, 2 tablespoons arugula. Press down firmly but gently and refrigerate until serving time.

To serve, slide a spatula under each stack cylinder and transfer to a serving plate. Garnish with 2 tablespoons crumbled Gorgonzola and 2 teaspoons pecans, drizzle with vinaigrette, and serve.

CANDIED PECANS

YIELD: ABOUT $2^1/_2$ CUPS

$^3/_4$ cup sugar

$^1/_4$ cup water

1 teaspoon ground cinnamon

$^1/_8$ teaspoon ground cloves

1 teaspoon white corn syrup

$^1/_8$ teaspoon salt

$2^1/_2$ cups pecan halves

In a large saucepan, bring sugar, water, cinnamon, cloves, corn syrup, and salt to a boil. Boil for 5 minutes. Add the nuts and stir for 30 seconds. Pour out onto a wax paper–lined sheet pan, separate with a fork, and let cool. Keeps for 1 month stored in an airtight container.

PEAR-HONEY VINAIGRETTE

YIELD: ABOUT $1^1/_2$ CUPS

1 ripe pear, soft but not mushy, peeled and seeded

2 tablespoons honey mustard

$^1/_2$ cup Japanese seasoned rice vinegar

1 tablespoon freshly squeezed lemon juice

$^1/_2$ teaspoon ground star anise

$^1/_4$ teaspoon ground cinnamon

$^1/_4$ teaspoon vanilla

$^1/_2$ cup canola oil

Combine the pear, mustard, vinegar, lemon juice, anise, cinnamon, and vanilla in a food processor and blend until smooth. Slowly add the oil while the machine is running and blend well.

Warm Sausage–Herb Potato Salad Stacks

Served warm or cold, this potato salad stack is my version of comfort food. Men love these! These stacks are also great for a light dinner or a picnic. Serve with a green salad and fruit for dessert.

Planning Ahead

• Prepare the stacks several hours ahead, without baking them, and chill.

• Prepare the vinaigrette the day before.

6 White Rose potatoes

²/₃ cup Dijon Vinaigrette (recipe follows)

Salt and freshly ground black pepper to taste

6 tablespoons chopped fresh parsley

6 tablespoons chopped fresh chives

²/₃ cup diced whole green onions

3 sweet Italian sausages

³/₄ cup grated Asiago cheese

Advance Preparation

Boil or steam the potatoes for 20 minutes or until cooked through. Peel and dice the potatoes while still warm, and place them in a bowl. Spoon 5 tablespoons vinaigrette over the potatoes. Sprinkle with salt and pepper and toss well. Set aside.

Mix together the parsley, chives, and green onions.

Grill, broil, or sauté the sausages, and slice about ¹/₄ inch thick.

Assembly

Preheat the oven to 350°.

Spray 6 stack cylinders with vegetable spray and place them on a sheet pan. Layer in the following order: 3 tablespoons potato, 1 tablespoon Asiago cheese, 4 slices sausage, 1 tablespoon parsley-chive-onion mixture. Repeat the layers and top with a third layer of potato. Press down gently but firmly. Bake for 10 minutes.

To serve, slide a spatula under each stack cylinder and transfer to a serving plate. Unmold, garnish with the remaining chopped parsley, chives, and green onions, drizzle with the remaining vinaigrette, and serve.

Note: This salad is also great cold or room temperature. After baking, chill salads for several hours. At serving time, unmold on a bed of baby greens and drizzle with dressing.

DIJON VINAIGRETTE
YIELD: ABOUT 1 CUP

2 cloves garlic, minced

2 shallots, minced

2 tablespoons Dijon mustard

$^1/_4$ cup sherry wine vinegar

Salt and freshly ground black pepper to taste

$^3/_4$ cup extra virgin olive oil

Mix together the garlic, shallots, mustard, vinegar, salt, and pepper and whisk until blended. Slowly add the oil, whisking, until the dressing is thick and well blended.

Shortcut Stacks
Purchase a quality Dijon vinaigrette.

Asparagus, Risotto, and Blood Oranges with Blood Orange Vinaigrette

This is an impressive salad stack, one that would be perfect for a luncheon or a light summer meal. To make it more substantial, try adding cooked cold lobster, crab, or shrimp.

Planning Ahead

• Prepare the asparagus, oranges, and vinaigrette the day before.

• Assemble and chill stacks 2 hours ahead.

RISOTTO

4 cups chicken stock (page 161)

1/2 cup freshly squeezed orange juice

3 tablespoons butter

1 1/2 cups arborio rice

Zest of 1 orange

5 tablespoons freshly grated Parmesan cheese

1 tablespoon minced fresh tarragon

16 spears fresh asparagus, trimmed and diced

4 blood oranges, peeled and sliced into 12 rounds total (see Note)

6 Bibb lettuce leaves

Blood Orange Vinaigrette (recipe follows)

Advance Preparation

To make the risotto, heat the chicken stock to a simmer. Heat the orange juice to a simmer. In a large saucepan, melt 2 tablespoons of the butter over medium-high heat and stir in the arborio rice. Cook, stirring to coat the rice, for 1 minute. Adjust the heat to medium. Pour 1 cup of hot stock over the rice and stir until all the liquid is absorbed. (The rice should be bubbling but not boiling furiously.) Continue adding stock 1/2 cup at a time and allowing it to be absorbed by the rice before adding more. Stir continually. After 10 minutes, add the hot orange juice and continue cooking and stirring. Add the orange zest. Cook the rice for an additional 8 minutes, adding stock as needed. When ready, the rice should be al dente or firm to the bite and cooked through. Do not overcook or the rice will become mushy. Remove the risotto from the heat and stir in the Parmesan, the additional 1 tablespoon butter, tarragon, and salt and pepper to taste.

To prepare the asparagus, blanch the asparagus in boiling water for 2 to 3 minutes, drain, and plunge into ice water.

Assembly

Spray 6 stack cylinders with vegetable spray and place them on a sheet pan. Layer in the following order: $1^1/_2$ tablespoons risotto, 1 tablespoon asparagus, $1^1/_2$ tablespoons risotto, 1 orange slice. Repeat the layers. Press down gently but firmly and chill for 1 hour or longer.

To serve, slide a spatula under each stack cylinder and transfer to a serving plate lined with a lettuce leaf. Unmold, drizzle with vinaigrette, sprinkle with additional orange zest, if you desire, and serve.

Note: If you have difficulty finding blood oranges, use navel oranges as a substitute.

BLOOD ORANGE VINAIGRETTE

YIELD: ABOUT 1 CUP

Juice and zest of 1 blood orange (see Note)

$^1/_3$ cup champagne vinegar

1 tablespoon orange marmalade

$^2/_3$ cup extra virgin olive oil

1 teaspoon minced fresh tarragon

Salt and freshly ground black pepper to taste

Whisk together the orange juice, vinegar, and marmalade. Slowly add the oil while whisking. Blend well. Add the orange zest, tarragon, salt, and pepper and blend.

Spinach, Mango, and Goat Cheese Stacks

The natural vitamins and minerals in fresh spinach make this an extremely healthy salad, and one we should consume at home on a weekly basis. Mangos are perfect with spinach and create a colorful presentation. Try substituting Brie for the goat cheese for a different flavor.

TIP: To peel a mango, cut the fruit lengthwise around the circumference. Peel half and slice the fruit off. Then peel the remaining side and slice. Peeling just one side at a time allows you a better grip on the fruit.

Planning Ahead

- This salad can be prepared 4 hours ahead.

- The vinaigrette can be made the day before, covered, and chilled.

8 to 10 ounces goat cheese, cut into
   $1/_4$-inch slices (18 slices)

6 cups fresh spinach, washed, stemmed,
   dried, and chopped

3 fresh mangoes, peeled, seeded, and diced

$1/_2$ cup sliced toasted almonds,
   (page 161)

$1/_2$ cup dried cranberries or cherries

$2/_3$ cup Mango Vinaigrette (recipe follows)

Assembly

Spray 6 stack cylinders with vegetable spray and place them on a sheet pan. Fit $1^1/_2$ slices of goat cheese on the bottom of the cylinder, so that the cheese covers the bottom. Layer in the following order: $1/_2$ cup spinach, 2 tablespoons mango, 2 teaspoons almonds, 2 teaspoons cranberries, $1^1/_2$ slices goat cheese. Repeat, ending with the almonds and cranberries. Press down firmly but gently and refrigerate 1 hour or longer (up to 4 hours).

To serve, slide a spatula under each stack cylinder and transfer to a serving plate. Unmold, drizzle with vinaigrette, sprinkle with any additional almonds, cranberries, and diced mango and serve.

MANGO VINAIGRETTE
YIELD: 2 CUPS

1 mango, peeled, seeded, and diced

2 tablespoons honey mustard

1 tablespoon mango chutney

$1/2$ cup Japanese seasoned rice wine vinegar

2 tablespoons freshly squeezed lime juice

2 teaspoons grated fresh ginger

$1/2$ cup canola or light vegetable oil

2 teaspoons poppy seeds

To make the vinaigrette, place the mango, mustard, chutney, vinegar, lime juice, and ginger in a food processor and blend until smooth. With the machine running, slowly add the oil, blending until slightly thickened. Stir in the poppy seeds. Refrigerate, covered, for up to 1 week.

Shortcut Stacks
Replace the Mango Vinaigrette with Consorzio Mango Vinaigrette, available in most fine markets.

Spinach-Sausage Stacks

YIELD: 6 SERVINGS

My friend Karen Betson gave me a recipe that sparked the idea for this salad stack. I added the grilled onions and goat cheese, which blend beautifully with the spinach and sausage, but the taste award goes to Karen.

Planning Ahead

- Sauté the sausage, shallots, and garlic early in the day and reheat prior to serving.
- Prepare the warm dressing early and reheat prior to serving.
- Grill the onion slices early in the day. Set aside.

3 onions, sliced $1/4$ inch thick (12 slices)

$1/4$ cup olive oil

8 ounces Italian garlic sausage, andouille, sweet Italian sausage, or Linguica

2 shallots, diced

2 cloves garlic, minced

$1/4$ cup balsamic vinegar

1 tablespoon sugar

Salt and freshly ground black pepper to taste

3 tablespoons extra virgin olive oil

3 cups fresh spinach, washed, trimmed, chilled, and coarsely chopped

18 slices goat cheese (about 12 ounces)

Advance Preparation

To make the onions, brush the onion slices lightly with olive oil and place on a hot barbecue grill or a stovetop grill pan. Cook until lightly browned, about 4 minutes. Turn and cook the other side.

To make the sausage, chop the sausage in a food processor and place in a large heated skillet with the shallots and garlic. Sauté until the sausage is broken up and browned, about 10 minutes. Remove with a slotted spoon and keep warm.

To make the dressing, pour out all but 3 tablespoons of sausage drippings. Add the vinegar, sugar, salt, pepper, and oil and blend well. Reduce for 3 minutes over medium heat, remove from the heat, and keep warm.

Assembly

Spray 6 stack cylinders with vegetable spray and place them on 6 serving plates. Layer in the following order: 1 grilled onion slice, $1/4$ cup spinach, 2 tablespoons sausage-shallot-garlic mix, $1^{1}/_{2}$ slices goat cheese. Drizzle with 1 tablespoon warm dressing. Then repeat the layers. Press down gently but firmly.

To serve, unmold, drizzle with additional warmed dressing, and serve immediately.

Shortcut Stacks

Purchase ready-cut and trimmed fresh spinach.

Ahi Niçoise Salad Stacks

YIELD: 6 SERVINGS

A terrific entrée salad for hot summer nights! The classic Salade Niçoise gets a facelift with a stack version made with grilled ahi.

Planning Ahead

- Prep all ingredients, except the ahi, the day before.
- Assemble the stacks and chill 3 hours ahead.
- Prepare the dressing the day before.

TIP: To test olive oil for freshness: place a small amount ($1/2$ teaspoon) in the palm of your hand. Quickly and briskly rub your hands together, then hold them, cupped, over your nose. If the oil smells fruity and clean, it is fresh. Always purchase olive oil in small (up to 25-ounce) glass bottles and store it in a cool, dark place.

AHI

2 pounds fresh ahi

1 cup Balsamic Glaze (recipe follows)

DRESSING

2 tablespoons freshly squeezed lemon juice

1 clove garlic, minced

3 anchovy fillets, minced

1 teaspoon Colman's mustard powder

$1/2$ cup Japanese seasoned rice wine vinegar

$1/2$ cup extra virgin olive oil

3 tablespoons chopped fresh parsley

Salt and freshly ground black pepper to taste

SALAD

3 large or 4 medium White Rose potatoes

1 cup French green beans, trimmed

3 hard-boiled eggs, peeled and chopped

2 heirloom tomatoes or ripe red or yellow tomatoes, cut into 12 slices

$1/2$ cup niçoise olives, pitted and chopped

$1/4$ cup capers

3 cups mixed spinach, Bibb lettuce, and romaine lettuce, washed, dried, and torn into pieces

Advance Preparation

To make the ahi, marinate the ahi in the glaze for 20 minutes. Drain and grill quickly over hot coals, or broil, to rare (about 2 minutes per side). The fish should be seared on the outside and pink on the inside. Thinly slice the ahi across the grain into $1/_4$-inch-thick slices. You should have approximately 36 slices. Set aside.

To make the dressing, combine the lemon juice, garlic, anchovies, mustard, and vinegar in a food processor and blend well. Slowly add the oil with the machine running and blend until emulsified. Stir in the parsley, salt, and pepper.

Boil the potatoes in salted water (to cover) for 15 to 20 minutes, or until a knife easily pierces the center of the potatoes. Drain, peel, and slice $1/_4$ inch thick.

To prepare the green beans, boil them for 3 minutes in salted water (to cover). Then drain and chop the beans.

Assembly

Spray 6 stack cylinders with vegetable spray and place them on a sheet pan. Layer the stacks in the following order: 1 layer of sliced potatoes, 2 tablespoons green beans, 3 ahi slices (to cover beans), 1 tablespoon egg, 1 slice tomato, 2 teaspoons olives, 1 teaspoon capers. Repeat the layers and top with a third layer of potatoes, overlapping the slices decoratively. Press down gently but firmly and chill 1 hour or longer, up to 3 hours.

To serve, slide a spatula under each stack cylinder and transfer to a serving plate lined with mixed lettuces. Unmold the stack, drizzle with dressing, and serve immediately.

BALSAMIC GLAZE
YIELD: 2 CUPS

$1/_4$ teaspoon ground star anise

$1 1/_2$ cups water

$1/_2$ cup sugar

$1/_2$ cup balsamic vinegar

Combine all the ingredients and boil for 10 minutes. Remove from the heat and allow to cool. Keeps in the refrigerator several weeks.

Note: This syrup is also terrific when used as a marinade for grilled chicken, onions, and eggplant. For a fabulous dessert, marinate strawberries in Balsamic Glaze and stack with pound cake and vanilla ice cream.

Eggplant-Salmon Salad Stacks

YIELD: 6 SERVINGS

The first time I experienced "tall" food was at the Parkway Grill in Pasadena, California. The chef created what he called "Tiki Salad." It had all of these wonderful flavors. After trying to obtain the recipe and not getting anywhere, I decided to attempt my own version. Mine doesn't come close to the original, but I hope I have honored it.

Planning Ahead

• Prepare the eggplant, salsa, relish, potatoes, and dressings the day before.

• Assemble the stacks just before serving, so the potatoes and salmon are still warm.

2 large eggplants, cut into 24 $1/4$-inch slices

$1/2$ cup olive oil

$1/3$ cup balsamic vinegar

$1^1/_2$ pounds fresh salmon fillet

3 cups Garlic Mashed Potatoes (page 163)

3 cups baby lettuces, slightly chopped

$1^1/_2$ cups Tomato Relish (recipe follows)

$1^1/_2$ cups Mango Salsa (recipe follows)

6 tablespoons Soy-Sesame Dressing (recipe follows)

6 tablespoons Papaya Dressing (recipe follows)

24 long chives, for garnish

1 mango, diced, for garnish

Advance Preparation

To make the eggplant, lightly brush the eggplant slices with olive oil. Place on a medium-hot grill and cook for 2 to 3 minutes per side, or until the eggplant is golden brown and soft. Sprinkle lightly with balsamic vinegar. Set aside.

To make the salmon, place the salmon on a medium-hot grill and cook for 4 to 5 minutes per side, or until the center is no longer rare. Do not overcook. Flake the salmon with a fork and set aside.

Eggplant–Salmon Salad Stacks cont.

Assembly

Spray 6 stack cylinders with vegetable spray and place them on 6 serving plates. Layer in the following order: 1 slice eggplant, trimmed to fit cylinder, 3 tablespoons warm mashed potatoes, 2 tablespoons baby lettuces, 1 tablespoon Tomato Relish, 1 slice eggplant, 1 tablespoon Mango Salsa, 2 tablespoons salmon. Repeat. Press down gently but firmly to compact the layers.

To serve, unmold the salad, spoon 1 tablespoon Soy-Sesame Dressing and 1 tablespoon Papaya Dressing around the base of the salad, garnish with long chives and diced mango, and serve immediately.

MANGO SALSA
YIELD: 1 1/2 CUPS

1 mango, peeled and diced

2 tablespoons chopped cilantro

1/4 cup peeled, seeded, and diced cucumber

1/4 cup diced red bell pepper

2 tablespoons diced red onion

1 tablespoon freshly squeezed lime juice

1/8 teaspoon crushed red pepper flakes

Mix all of the ingredients together and chill. The salsa can be made several hours in advance.

TOMATO RELISH
YIELD: 2 CUPS

3 plum tomatoes, seeded and diced

1 tablespoon chopped cilantro

1/4 cup diced whole green onions

1 to 2 tablespoons diced jalapeño (fresh or canned)

1 tablespoon sherry vinegar

1/4 cup extra virgin olive oil

1 teaspoon chopped fresh basil

1 tablespoon chopped fresh parsley

Salt and freshly ground black pepper to taste

Mix all of the ingredients together and chill. The relish can be made several hours in advance.

Soy–Sesame Dressing

YIELD: $^2/_3$ CUP

2 tablespoons sesame oil

$^1/_4$ teaspoon crushed red pepper flakes

1 tablespoon minced fresh ginger

1 clove garlic, minced

$^1/_4$ cup hoisin sauce

2 tablespoons balsamic vinegar

2 tablespoons soy sauce

2 tablespoons freshly squeezed orange juice

1 teaspoon ground coriander

$^1/_2$ teaspoon five-spice powder

Heat the oil in a small skillet. Add the pepper flakes and cook 30 seconds. Add the ginger and garlic and sauté 1 minute on medium-low heat. Do not burn the garlic. Pour the warm garlic-ginger oil into a bowl and add the remaining ingredients. Blend well. Serve warm or at room temperature. Can be made 2 days in advance.

Papaya Dressing

YIELD: 2 CUPS

1 cup Consorzio Passion Fruit Vinaigrette

2 tablespoons freshly squeezed lime juice

$^1/_2$ papaya, peeled (rinse and reserve half the seeds)

$^1/_4$ vanilla bean, split and seeds removed

1 tablespoon honey

3 tablespoons vegetable oil

Place all of the ingredients, including the reserved papaya seeds, in a food processor and blend well. Chill. Can be made 2 to 3 days in advance.

Shortcut Stacks

- Purchase the mashed potatoes and poached salmon at your local deli or gourmet shop.

- Purchase a fresh mild tomato salsa.

- Purchase a Chinese chicken-salad dressing in place of the Soy-Sesame Dressing.

Zucchini-Apple Salad Stacks

YIELD: 6 SERVINGS

The crunchy texture of this salad is really appealing and healthy. Apples and jicama work well together, and the zucchini "ribbons" give this stack a whimsical look. Try this for a ladies' luncheon or bridal shower.

Planning Ahead

- Prepare the stacks 3 hours ahead and chill.
- Prepare the vinaigrette the day before.
- Prepare the zucchini ribbons in the morning and place them in ice water and refrigerate.
- Slice the apple garnish at the last minute.

TIP: Zucchini ribbons are made by running a vegetable peeler the length of the zucchini. To curl, place rolled up zucchini ribbons in ice water for an hour or longer. Drain and use the "curled" ribbons as garnish.

1 small jicama, peeled and coarsely chopped

2 Red Delicious, Granny Smith, or Fuji apples, coarsely chopped

$1/2$ cup Lemon-Currant Vinaigrette (recipe follows)

2 medium zucchini, very thinly sliced

3 cups red leaf lettuce, torn into small pieces

8 ounces Maytag blue cheese, crumbled

1 apple, very thinly sliced, for garnish

Juice of 1 lemon

2 medium zucchini, made into about 18 "ribbons" for garnish (see Tip)

Advance Preparation

Combine the jicama and apples with just enough vinaigrette to moisten.

Assembly

Spray 6 stack cylinders with vegetable spray and place them on a sheet pan. Layer in the following order: 1 layer of overlapping zucchini slices, $^1/_4$ cup red leaf lettuce, 2 tablespoons jicama-apple mixture, 1 tablespoon blue cheese. Repeat the layers and top with a third layer of zucchini slices. Press down gently but firmly and chill for 1 hour or longer.

To serve, slide a spatula under each stack cylinder and transfer to a serving plate. Unmold and drizzle with Lemon-Currant Vinaigrette. Brush the thin apple slices with lemon juice. Garnish with the apple slices and zucchini ribbons and serve.

LEMON–CURRANT VINAIGRETTE
YIELD: ABOUT $^3/_4$ CUP

Juice of 1 lemon

1 tablespoon champagne vinegar

$^1/_2$ teaspoon Colman's mustard powder

1 teaspoon honey

Dash of salt

$^1/_2$ cup vegetable oil

2 teaspoons minced fresh parsley

1$^1/_2$ tablespoons currants

Whisk together the lemon juice, vinegar, mustard, honey, and salt. Slowly add the oil while whisking and blend well. Stir in the parsley and currants. Let stand at room temperature for 1 hour to allow flavors to blend.

Gazpacho Salad Stacks

YIELD: 6 SERVINGS

I created this salad when teaching in my cooking school, Mama's Cookin' Company. We would all gather in my home, drink wine, learn a menu, then eat what we made. My friend Judy Schoenfeld had to bring her husband one night because he didn't believe a cooking class could last until midnight!

Planning Ahead

- Prepare and drain all the vegetables the day before. (The secret to this salad is uniformly diced and drained vegetables.)

- Prepare the dressing the day before.

- Assemble the stacks 2 hours ahead and chill.

- Prepare the minced parsley early in the day.

1 green bell pepper, seeded and diced

1 red bell pepper, seeded and diced

$1/2$ red onion, diced

2 stalks celery, diced

1 teaspoon red wine vinegar

$1/4$ teaspoon sugar

3 cups small croutons

$1 1/2$ avocados, peeled, pitted, and diced

2 cups peeled, seeded, and diced tomatoes, drained

1 English cucumber, peeled, seeded, diced, and drained

3 whole green onions, diced

6 tablespoons minced fresh parsley

Garlic-Lemon Dressing (recipe follows)

12 kalamata olives, pitted and chopped, for garnish

$1/2$ cup capers, for garnish

6 anchovies, diced, for garnish

Advance Preparation

Toss the peppers, onion, and celery with vinegar and sugar. Set aside.

Assembly

Spray 6 stack cylinders with vegetable spray and place them on a parchment-lined sheet pan. Layer in the following order: $1/4$ cup croutons, 2 tablespoons pepper-onion-celery mixture, 1 tablespoon avocado, 2 tablespoons tomatoes, 2 tablespoons cucumbers, 1 teaspoon green onions, 1 teaspoon parsley. Repeat the layers. Press down gently but firmly and chill for 1 to 2 hours.

To serve, slide a spatula under each stack cylinder and transfer to a serving plate. Unmold and drizzle dressing over and around stack. Garnish with olives, capers, anchovies, and 2 tablespoons minced parsley and serve.

GARLIC-LEMON DRESSING
YIELD: ABOUT $2/3$ CUP

3 cloves garlic, peeled

1 teaspoon salt

Zest of 1 lemon

2 tablespoons fresh basil

3 teaspoons Dijon mustard

3 tablespoons freshly squeezed lemon juice

Dash of Tabasco sauce

Freshly ground black pepper to taste

$1/2$ cup extra virgin olive oil

Combine the garlic salt, lemon zest, basil, mustard, lemon juice, Tabasco, and pepper in a food processor and blend well. Slowly add the oil while the machine is running, until the dressing is well blended and thickened. Can be made ahead and refrigerated.

Rock Shrimp and Asparagus Sushi Stacks

SEAFOOD STACKS

Rock Shrimp and Asparagus Sushi Stacks

YIELD: 6 SERVINGS

I came up with these stacks while trying to come up with a clever first course for a picnic. They travel beautifully and are perfect as chilled summer fare. For picnics carry the sauce in a jar. Take along wasabi, ginger, chives, and sesame seeds for the garnish. If you have an unusual mold shape—a pyramid, triangle, or square—use it. These stacks look great in interesting shapes. Then get ready to take a bow.

Planning Ahead

- Just about every layer can be prepped ahead. Cut the avocado just before layering the stacks.

- Sushi stacks do very well when layered as much as 6 hours ahead, leaving you time to attend to the rest of the meal. The sauce can be made several days in advance and chilled, covered.

TIP: When cooling sushi rice, to achieve that glossy look, use a fan or a hairdryer set on "cool" to speed the cooling process. Fan the bowl of warm rice while adding the vinegar. This produces a beautiful sheen to the rice.

ROCK SHRIMP

$1^1/_2$ pounds rock shrimp, rinsed, drained, and patted dry

1 tablespoon vegetable oil

1 clove garlic

1 tablespoon mirin (Japanese sweet wine)

ASPARAGUS

$1^1/_4$ pounds fresh asparagus spears

1 cup mayonnaise

1 tablespoon Thai garlic-chile paste

1 tablespoon orange fish roe (*tobiko*)

2 tablespoons minced whole green onions

1 teaspoon freshly squeezed lemon juice

$3/_4$ cup orange fish roe (*tobiko*)

3 cups sushi rice (page 162)

2 tablespoons wasabi paste, plus additional for garnish

$2/_3$ cup diced avocado

$3/_4$ cup chopped radish sprouts

18 sprigs chives

$1/_2$ cup Sesame-Peanut Sauce (recipe follows)

1 tablespoon black sesame seeds (optional), for garnish

6 tablespoons pickled ginger, for garnish

Advance Preparation

To prepare the rock shrimp, sauté the shrimp in the vegetable oil over high heat for about 2 minutes. Add the garlic and sauté 1 minute. Add the mirin and cook until all juices are evaporated. Chop the mixture and set aside.

To make the asparagus, blanch the asparagus for 1 minute. Drain the asparagus. Then trim and chop it. Combine the mayonnaise, garlic-chile paste, 1 tablespoon roe, green onions, and lemon juice. Mix the asparagus with the sauce. Set aside.

Assembly

Spray 6 stack cylinders or pyramid molds with vegetable spray and place them on a sheet pan. Layer in the following order: 2 tablespoons roe, 2 tablespoons sushi rice, $1/8$ teaspoon wasabi (spread over the rice), 2 tablespoons rock shrimp, 1 generous tablespoon avocado, 1 tablespoon roe, 2 tablespoons sushi rice, 2 tablespoons asparagus, 2 tablespoons radish sprouts, 2 tablespoons sushi rice. Press down firmly. Top each stack with 1 tablespoon asparagus. Chill until serving time.

If using a pyramid mold, line with plastic wrap and begin by placing 1 tablespoon of roe in the bottom, forming the "tip" of the pyramid.

To serve, slide a spatula under each stack and transfer to a serving plate. Unmold and garnish.

To garnish, poke a hole in the top of each stack with a skewer and arrange several chive sprigs coming out the top. Spoon sesame sauce around the base and sprinkle with sesame seeds. Garnish with more wasabi and pickled ginger.

SESAME PEANUT SAUCE
YIELD: ABOUT $1 1/2$ CUPS

- $1/2$ cup Thai peanut sauce
- $1/4$ cup soy sauce
- 3 tablespoons sesame oil
- $1/2$ cup Japanese seasoned rice wine vinegar
- 1 tablespoon toasted sesame seeds (page 161)
- 1 teaspoon grated fresh ginger

Mix all ingredients together and whisk to blend. Chill until serving time. Will keep for 1 week in the refrigerator.

Shortcut Stacks

- Buy the sushi rice from a local Japanese restaurant or a deli that makes fresh sushi, instead of making your own.

- Buy spicy sushi mayonnaise, a type of mayonnaise sauce used in sushi bars, to mix with the asparagus.

Chinese Vegetables with Ahi and Sesame Vinaigrette

YIELD: 6 SERVINGS

Try this on your health-minded, fat-conscious friends—a great "spa stack." The vinaigrette is also great on a fresh spinach, sprout, and mushroom salad, or over blanched Asian vegetables.

Planning Ahead

- All the vegetables can be prepped the day before, covered, and chilled. Toss them in the vinaigrette about 1 hour before stacking.

- The vinaigrette can be made ahead of time and kept, covered, in the refrigerator for 1 week.

- Layer the stacks 2 to 3 hours ahead. They can be served cold or warmed in the oven just prior to serving.

- The garnish can be made early in the day and chilled.

AHI

3 pounds very fresh ahi tuna

3 tablespoons extra virgin olive oil

Salt and freshly ground black pepper to taste

SESAME VINAIGRETTE

$^1/_4$ cup soy sauce

$^1/_2$ cup Japanese seasoned rice wine vinegar

2 small shallots, chopped

2 tablespoons minced pickled ginger

1 teaspoon sugar

2 tablespoons Dijon mustard

1 tablespoon Asian chile–garlic sauce

1 clove garlic, chopped

1 teaspoon black sesame seeds

$^3/_4$ cup peanut oil

2 tablespoons sesame oil

VEGETABLES

3 baby bok choy, chopped

1 pound Chinese long beans or French green beans, cut into $1^1/_2$-inch lengths

24 asparagus tips

2 pounds fresh spinach, washed, stemmed, and diced

6 shiitake mushrooms, sliced

2 teaspoons peanut oil

3 cups sushi rice (page 162)

1 firm daikon radish, julienned, for garnish

1 container radish sprouts, washed and trimmed, for garnish

$1^1/_2$ tomatoes, peeled, seeded, and diced, for garnish

1 tablespoon black sesame seeds, for garnish

3 tablespoons wasabi paste, for garnish

6 tablespoons pickled ginger, for garnish

Advance Preparation

To make the ahi, brush the tuna with a little olive oil and grill over very hot coals for 1 to 3 minutes, until the outside is seared and the inside is still pink. Season with salt and pepper, slice across the grain, $^1/_4$ inch thick, and keep warm.

To make the vinaigrette, combine the soy sauce, vinegar, shallots, ginger, sugar, mustard, chile-garlic sauce, garlic, and sesame seeds in a food processor and blend for 30 seconds. Slowly add the oils with the machine running. Strain through a strainer and set aside.

To make the vegetables, blanch the bok choy, beans, asparagus, and spinach—1 vegetable at a time—in boiling salted water for 1 minute. Drain well. Sauté the mushrooms for 1 minute in the peanut oil over medium-high heat. Toss all the vegetables in 3 tablespoons of the vinaigrette. Set aside.

Assembly

Spray 6 stack cylinders with vegetable spray. Place a stack cylinder on each of 6 warm plates. Spoon $^1/_2$ cup sushi rice into each stack and press down. Spoon $^3/_4$ cup vegetables into each stack and press down firmly but gently. Unmold and arrange the sliced tuna around the vegetables.

To serve, top with a garnish of daikon and radish sprouts. Surround the stack with diced tomatoes, sesame seeds, wasabi, ginger, and additional vinaigrette. Serve immediately.

Note: You can use a Japanese vegetable cutter for the garnish. These nifty little gadgets are available at fine gourmet cookware stores everywhere (see Resources, page 169) and create long, thin strands of fresh daikon, carrots, and cucumber.

Shortcut Stacks

- Buy the sushi rice from a Japanese restaurant or sushi bar.
- Use a quality bottled sesame-soy dressing in place of the vinaigrette.
- Buy packaged fresh baby spinach.

Sweet Potato Pancakes with Rock Shrimp and Mango Syrup

YIELD: 6 SERVINGS

After learning to make potato latkes from my mother-in-law, Henny Fabricant, I became intrigued with the idea of different flavors and textures in pancakes. Sweet potatoes are perfect for little pancakes. They are easy to make, very tasty, and keep well.

Planning Ahead

- The potato pancakes can be made 2 hours ahead and kept warm in a very low oven.

- Have all the ingredients for the shrimp ready a day ahead. Stir-frying then becomes a 3-minute task.

- Make the Mango Syrup 2 to 3 days ahead and chill.

POTATO PANCAKES

$1/2$ pound Yukon Gold potatoes, peeled

$1 1/2$ pounds sweet potatoes, peeled

4 tablespoons melted butter

Salt and freshly ground pepper to taste

ROCK SHRIMP

2 tablespoons extra virgin olive oil

2 pounds rock shrimp, rinsed, drained, and patted dry

3 ears fresh corn, cleaned and kernels removed

8 whole green onions, chopped

$1/2$ teaspoon salt

Freshly ground pepper to taste

1 pint yellow and red teardrop tomatoes or cherry tomatoes, halved

$1/4$ cup heavy whipping cream

MANGO SYRUP

2 fresh mangoes, peeled, seeded, and chopped

$1/4$ teaspoon allspice

$1/2$ cup chutney

Pinch of cayenne

$1/4$ teaspoon cinnamon

1 teaspoon sugar

$1/2$ teaspoon salt

$1/2$ cup Japanese seasoned rice wine vinegar

1 tablespoon freshly squeezed lemon juice

3 tablespoons fresh chives, for garnish

3 tablespoons diced mango, for garnish

2 tablespoons minced fresh parsley, for garnish

Advance Preparation

To make the potato pancakes, shred the potatoes and sweet potatoes using the large holes on a handheld grater or the shredding disc of a food processor. Do not rinse. Pat dry to remove any natural moisture. Mix the potatoes with the melted butter and add salt and pepper to taste. Heat a large nonstick skillet, spray it with vegetable spray or wipe with a little oil or butter, and drop $1/4$-cup mounds of potatoes onto the hot skillet. With the back of a spatula, press down on each mound, flattening it to a 3-inch circle. Cook over medium-high heat until the underside is crisp and brown. Flip the pancakes with a spatula and cook the other side until crisp and brown. Remove to a warm plate or sheet pan. Repeat for the remaining potato batter. The potatoes can be kept warm in a low oven for 1 to 2 hours. You will need a total of 18 pancakes.

To make the shrimp, heat the olive oil in a large skillet over high heat. Add the shrimp and sauté for 1 minute, until the shrimp is pink. Add the corn and green onions and sauté 3 minutes. Add the salt, pepper, tomatoes, and cream. Cook for a few minutes to thicken the cream. Keep warm.

To make the syrup, place all the syrup ingredients in a food processor and blend until thick and smooth. Warm before using.

Assembly

These are free-form stacks. To make the stacks, place a potato pancake on each of 6 serving plates. Top with $1/4$ cup rock shrimp mixture. Repeat, ending with a third potato pancake.

To serve, warm the syrup. Spoon syrup around stacks. Garnish with chives, diced mango, and parsley.

Shortcut Stacks

Make the stacks with couscous, rice, or mashed sweet potatoes, instead of the potato pancakes.

Grilled Salmon and Corn Pancake Stacks

YIELD: 6 SERVINGS

Another twist on the pancake free-form stack, this dish using sugar snap peas and tomatoes has a wonderful color and texture. Try stacking corn pancakes with ham or barbecued chicken cut from the bone and diced.

Planning Ahead

- The pancake batter can be made a day ahead and chilled.
- The pancakes can be cooked 1 hour ahead and kept warm in an oven on very low heat.
- Prepare the vegetables early in the day and assemble the remaining ingredients. It will only take a moment to stir-fry.
- Have the garnish ready.

CORN PANCAKES

2 eggs

$1^3/_4$ cups whole milk

1 cup sifted all-purpose flour

4 teaspoons baking powder

1 teaspoon sugar

1 teaspoon salt

$1/_4$ teaspoon freshly ground black pepper

2 ears fresh corn, cleaned and kernels removed (about 1 cup)

4 tablespoons chopped chives

$1/_2$ teaspoon butter

SALMON

2 pounds fresh salmon fillet

3 tablespoons extra virgin olive oil

$1/_2$ cup crème fraîche, plus additional for garnish

2 bunches watercress, washed, trimmed, and dried

Tomato–Snap Pea Garnish (recipe follows)

2 ounces golden caviar (optional)

Advance Preparation

To make the corn pancakes, whip the eggs. Then add the milk, flour, baking powder, sugar, salt, and pepper and blend well with a whisk. Stir in the corn kernels and chives. Heat a large, flat skillet or griddle and brush with butter. With a $1^1/_2$-ounce (3-tablespoon) ladle, pour the batter onto the hot griddle, forming 3-inch pancakes. Cook until bubbles form on the top and the edges of the pancakes begin to look dry. Flip the pancakes over and cook for about 1 minute. Transfer to a warm, parchment-lined sheet pan. You will need 18 pancakes.

To make the salmon, brush the salmon with a thin coat of olive oil and grill it over hot coals or under the broiler until the fish is just cooked inside, about 6 to 8 minutes. Keep warm.

Assembly

To assemble the stacks, place a corn pancake on each of 6 serving plates. Frost with $1^1/_2$ teaspoons crème fraîche. Top with 3 tablespoons flaked salmon and top the salmon with 3 tablespoons watercress. Repeat twice, using 3 pancakes per serving, ending with the watercress.

To serve, spoon the Tomato–Snap Pea Garnish around each stack and garnish with golden caviar and additional crème fraîche, if desired.

Shortcut Stacks

Layer the stacks in cylinders with cooked brown rice, mashed potatoes, or cooked quinoa. Using any of these "binders" and layering in cylinders, you can make the stacks 3 to 4 hours ahead and chill. Bake at 350° for 10 to 15 minutes prior to serving.

TOMATO–SNAP PEA GARNISH

1 tablespoon butter

2 cloves garlic, minced

1 pint baby pear tomatoes, cherry tomatoes, yellow baby pear tomatoes, or a combination, halved

2 cups sugar snap peas, stemmed

4 whole green onions, chopped

$1/_2$ cup white wine

Salt and freshly ground black pepper to taste

Melt the butter in a large skillet over medium-high heat. Add the garlic and cook 30 seconds, being careful not to burn. Add the tomatoes, sugar snap peas, and green onions and cook over medium heat for about 3 minutes, stirring. Add the white wine, increase the heat, and cook for 2 more minutes. Season with salt and pepper. Keep warm.

Shrimp Cake Stacks

YIELD: 6 SERVINGS

I liked the idea of shrimp cakes for stacks and decided to experiment with layers of shrimp cake mixture and asparagus. It was good, but needed another element plus some color, which I found in the sweet potato purée. This combination has won rave reviews from my friends at dinner parties.

Planning Ahead

- Prepare the shrimp, pack it into the cylinders early in the day, and chill.
- Prepare the sweet potatoes and keep them warm in a double boiler—up to 2 hours ahead.
- Prepare the salsa 2 to 4 hours ahead and chill.

SHRIMP CAKES

3 tablespoons butter

1 tablespoon extra virgin olive oil

$1/_3$ cup chopped green onions

$1/_3$ cup chopped shallots

$1/_4$ cup chopped red bell pepper

$1/_4$ cup chopped yellow bell pepper

$1^1/_2$ pounds raw shrimp, peeled, deveined, and chopped

$1/_2$ pound small scallops, chopped

1 ear fresh corn, cleaned and kernels removed

$1^1/_2$ cups fresh bread crumbs

3 small eggs, beaten

1 teaspoon minced fresh thyme

$1/_4$ teaspoon paprika

2 tablespoons chopped fresh cilantro

ASPARAGUS

2 pounds asparagus (about 40 spears), washed and stemmed

1 tablespoon extra virgin olive oil

$1/_3$ cup chopped shallots

SWEET POTATO PURÉE

2 sweet potatoes

1 tablespoon butter

Pinch of cardamom

Salt and freshly ground black pepper to taste

1 tablespoon extra virgin olive oil

Mango-Orange Salsa (recipe follows)

2 tablespoons minced fresh parsley, for garnish (optional)

2 tablespoons minced fresh thyme, for garnish (optional)

6 tablespoons minced mango

Advance Preparation

To make the shrimp cakes, melt the butter with the olive oil in a large skillet and sauté the green onions, shallots, and peppers until soft. Cool slightly. Mix together the onion-pepper mixture with the shrimp, scallops, corn, bread crumbs, eggs, thyme, paprika, and cilantro. Set aside.

To make the asparagus, dice 20 asparagus spears and sauté in the olive oil with the shallots until just cooked through but still crisp, about 4 minutes. Set aside.

To make the sweet potato purée, preheat the oven to 375°. Bake the sweet potatoes for 45 minutes, or until soft. Cut them in half and scoop out the soft insides. Mix with butter, cardamom, and salt and pepper. Whip until smooth and keep warm.

Assembly

Preheat oven to 375°.

Spray 6 stack cylinders with vegetable spray and place them on a sheet pan. Spread $1/4$ cup shrimp mixture on the bottom of each cylinder and then a layer of asparagus. Repeat the layers and top with a third layer of shrimp. Press down firmly. In a large ovenproof skillet, heat 1 tablespoon olive oil over medium-high heat. Using a spatula, carefully transfer the stacks to the skillet and sauté for 3 minutes. Place the skillet and stacks in the oven and bake 15 minutes. Remove and let the stacks set for 5 minutes. The shrimp should feel firm to the touch. While stacks are setting, parboil the remaining asparagus spears until crisp-tender, about 3 minutes. Drain.

To serve, using a spatula, transfer each stack to 6 serving plates. Unmold, top each stack with a dollop of sweet potato purée, arrange 3 asparagus spears in a triangle around the base of each stack, and place a tablespoon of Mango-Orange Salsa at each corner. Sprinkle each with a little parsley, thyme, or mango and serve immediately.

MANGO-ORANGE SALSA
YIELD: ABOUT 3 CUPS

2 mangoes, peeled, pitted, and diced

$1/2$ avocado, peeled, pitted, and diced

$1/4$ pineapple, peeled, cored, and diced

3 tablespoons finely diced whole green onions

3 tablespoons chopped cilantro

1 orange, peeled and diced

$1/2$ red bell pepper, diced

$1^1/2$ tablespoons freshly squeezed lime juice

$1^1/2$ teaspoons grated fresh ginger

$1/4$ teaspoon red pepper flakes

Combine all of the ingredients and chill for 2 to 3 hours. Bring to room temperature before serving.

Note: This salsa is also wonderful with grilled chicken, pork, or seafood.

Ahi Sushi Stacks

Obviously, I like sushi! Don't be scared by this recipe. It is easy, delicious, and low in fat!

Planning Ahead

• Good news! These can be assembled, stacked, and chilled ahead of time and then reheated just prior to serving, leaving you only to worry about grilling the ahi.

• Plan to make the stacks early in the day.

• Make the Tamari-Chive Sauce 1 to 2 days ahead and chill.

TIP: Sushi stacks can be made in small (1$^{1}/_{2}$-inch) cylinders or tomato paste cans and served as appetizers.

2 pounds fresh ahi

3 tablespoons peanut oil

3 cups sushi rice (page 162)

1 tablespoon hot chile oil

15 shiitake mushrooms, sliced

4 cloves garlic, minced

$^{3}/_{4}$ cup bean sprouts

2 cups whole chopped green onions

6 baby bok choy, or 1 large bok choy, chopped

3 cloves garlic, minced

12 cups (approximately 3 large bunches) fresh spinach, washed, stemmed, and dried

1 teaspoon sesame oil

1 teaspoon black sesame seeds

TAMARI-CHIVE SAUCE

$^{1}/_{2}$ cup tamari (a mild soy sauce)

1 tablespoon freshly squeezed lemon juice

1 tablespoon sake

3 tablespoons Japanese seasoned rice wine vinegar

2 teaspoons sesame oil

2 tablespoons chopped chives

6 tablespoons pickled ginger, for garnish

2 tablespoons wasabi, for garnish (double that if you love wasabi)

Advance Preparation

To make the ahi, brush it with 1 tablespoon peanut oil and grill it over very hot coals until seared on the outside but still rare in the center, about 4 minutes. The ahi can be broiled under a very hot broiler for the same amount of time.

To make the vegetables and rice, prepare the sushi rice. Set aside. Heat 2 tablespoons peanut oil and chile oil in a large skillet or wok until very hot. Add the shiitakes, 4 cloves minced garlic, and bean sprouts. Stir-fry quickly until just cooked through, about 3 minutes. Remove with a slotted spoon. Set aside.

In the same pan, stir-fry the green onions and bok choy until just barely cooked, about 1 minute. Remove and set aside.

Just before serving, add a little more peanut oil (1 tablespoon) to the wok, if necessary. Add the 3 cloves minced garlic and sauté for a moment, then add the spinach and sauté until just barely wilted. Add the sesame oil and the sesame seeds. Divide the spinach between 6 serving plates.

To make the Tamari-Chive Sauce, combine the tamari, lemon juice, sake, and vinegar. Whisk in the oil. Stir in the chives.

Assembly

Preheat the oven to 400°.

Spray 6 stack cylinders with vegetable spray and place them on a sheet pan. Layer in the following order: 2 tablespoons sushi rice, 2 tablespoons shiitake mushrooms, 2 tablespoons sushi rice, 2 tablespoons bok choy and onion, 2 tablespoons sushi rice, 2 tablespoons shiitake mushrooms.

At this point the sushi stack can be refrigerated until serving time. Sushi stacks can be served cold or heated in a 400° oven for 10 minutes.

To serve, slide a spatula under each stack cylinder and transfer to a spinach-lined serving plate. Unmold and surround with fanned slices of the grilled ahi. Garnish with wasabi and pickled ginger, and serve.

Shortcut Stacks

- Buy prepared sushi rice from a good Japanese restaurant or sushi bar.

- Purchase stir-fried vegetables from a good Japanese restaurant and use in place of the shiitake layer and bok choy/onion layer.

Swordfish–Rosemary Polenta Stacks

YIELD: 6 SERVINGS

Swordfish is wonderful with Mediterranean flavors. The combination of polenta, rosemary, and swordfish is a winner.

Planning Ahead

- Make polenta rounds the day before and chill.
- Make the ratatouille the day before—being careful not to overcook.

TIP: Fish is fresh if it smells like the ocean, the eyes are bright and clear, the gills are reddish or pink, the scales bright and shiny, and the flesh is firm and springs back when touched.

2$^1/_2$ pounds swordfish steaks

2 tablespoons olive oil

POLENTA

1 (13$^1/_2$-ounce) package 5-minute polenta (page 164)

3 tablespoons butter

$^2/_3$ cup freshly grated Parmesan cheese

3 tablespoons chopped fresh rosemary

2 teaspoons salt

RATATOUILLE

6 tablespoons extra virgin olive oil

2$^1/_2$ cups diced eggplant

1 cup chopped onions

4 cloves garlic, minced

2 cups diced zucchini

1 cup diced red bell pepper

1 cup diced yellow bell pepper

3$^1/_2$ cups peeled, seeded, and diced tomatoes

10 basil leaves, julienned

$^1/_2$ cup marinated artichoke hearts, drained and chopped

Salt and freshly ground black pepper to taste

1 tablespoon fresh lemon juice

3 tablespoons minced fresh parsley, for garnish

$^1/_2$ cup freshly grated Parmesan cheese, for garnish

Advance Preparation

To make the swordfish, brush the swordfish steaks with olive oil and place over hot coals or under a high broiler flame. Cook a total of 8 minutes—4 minutes on each side. Coarsely chop the cooked swordfish.

To make the polenta, cook the polenta according to the directions on page 164, adding the butter, Parmesan, rosemary, and salt at the end. Mix well. Pour the polenta onto a lightly greased 12 by 17-inch sheet pan and smooth to $1/_2$ inch deep. Let rest for 20 minutes to firm up. When the polenta is firm, cut 16 3-inch rounds. (Use your stack cylinder as a cutting tool.) Set aside.

To make the ratatouille, heat the oil in a large frying pan. Add the eggplant and sauté until browned. Add the onions and garlic and sauté for about 3 minutes. Add the zucchini, peppers, and tomatoes and cook, stirring until the vegetables are just cooked through but not mushy, about 5 minutes. Add the basil, artichoke hearts, salt, and pepper and heat through. Stir in the lemon juice and remove from the heat.

Assembly

Preheat the oven to 350°.

Spray 6 stack cylinders with vegetable spray and place them on a greased sheet pan. Layer the stacks in the following order: 1 round of polenta, 3 tablespoons swordfish, 3 tablespoons ratatouille. Repeat the layers, ending with the ratatouille. Bake stacks for 10 minutes, or until heated through.

To serve, slide a spatula under each stack cylinder and transfer to a serving plate. Let the stacks rest a couple of minutes, then unmold.

Garnish with additional ratatouille, parsley, and Parmesan. Cut decorative shapes from the remaining polenta and place on stack tops.

Shortcut Stacks

Use polenta from the deli that comes in 3-inch diameter rolls. Just cut into $1/_2$-inch slices and layer the stacks. It's not as tasty as freshly prepared polenta, but it's easy if you're short on time.

Seafood Risotto Stacks

YIELD: 6 SERVINGS

This was one of the first stacks I made. I've always loved seafood risotto and, once I discovered how perfect risotto is in holding stack layers together, this was a natural. These stacks are great for a dinner party or luncheon.

Planning Ahead

- Early in the day, or the day before, prep the ingredients for the risotto. Prepare the spinach, tomatoes, asparagus, shrimp, and salmon and chill.

- Make the tomato sauce 1 to 2 days ahead and chill.

- Layer the stacks 1 to 2 hours before serving and chill. Bring to room temperature for a half hour before baking.

RISOTTO

1 cup clam broth

5 cups chicken stock

1 tablespoon butter

1 tablespoon extra virgin olive oil

1 cup diced whole green onions

3 cloves garlic, minced

$1^1/_2$ cups arborio rice

$^1/_2$ cup white wine

1 cup frozen peas

$^1/_2$ cup chopped fresh Italian parsley, plus additional for garnish

$^1/_2$ cup freshly grated Parmesan cheese

Salt and freshly ground black pepper to taste

1 teaspoon minced fresh thyme

$^1/_4$ teaspoon red pepper flakes

12 fresh asparagus spears

4 tablespoons olive oil

$^1/_2$ pound medium shrimp, peeled and deveined

$^1/_2$ pound fresh salmon

2 cups peeled, seeded, and chopped tomatoes

2 cups fresh spinach, washed, stemmed, dried, and chopped

$1^1/_2$ cups Italian Tomato Sauce (page 160)

Advance Preparation

To make the risotto, heat the clam broth and chicken stock to simmering.

Heat the butter and oil in a large saucepan or Dutch oven. Add the onions and garlic and sauté 1 minute. Add the rice and sauté 1 minute. Add the wine. Bring to a gentle boil and stir until all liquid is absorbed. Add $1/2$ cup of simmering chicken/clam stock. Stir over medium-high heat until liquid is absorbed, then add another $1/2$ cup. Continue in this fashion for a total of 18 minutes, allowing the liquid to absorb each time. When rice is cooked and liquid absorbed (you may not need all of the stock), add the peas, parsley, Parmesan, and seasonings. Stir for 1 minute. Remove from the heat and keep covered. Should the risotto become too stiff, add $1/4$ cup broth and stir before continuing with the stacks. (Do not allow it to become runny.)

To make the asparagus, chop spears and cook in boiling salted water for 3 minutes. Drain and refresh in ice water. Drain. Set aside.

To make the shrimp, lightly oil the shrimp and grill them over hot coals or broil them for a total of 5 minutes, or until pink and cooked through. Coarsely chop and set aside.

To make the salmon, lightly oil both sides and place over hot coals or broil for a total of 6 minutes, or until the salmon is just cooked through. Do not overcook. Chop and set aside.

Assembly

Preheat the oven to 375°.

Spray 6 stack cylinders with vegetable spray and place them on a sheet pan. Layer in the following order: 2 tablespoons risotto, 1 tablespoon asparagus, 2 tablespoons shrimp, 1 tablespoon tomato, 1 tablespoon spinach, 2 tablespoons risotto, 1 tablespoon asparagus, 2 tablespoons salmon, 1 tablespoon tomato, 1 tablespoon spinach, 2 tablespoons risotto. Press down gently but firmly to compact layers. Bake at 375° for 10 minutes. Let rest 2 to 3 minutes.

To serve, slide a spatula under each stack cylinder and transfer to a serving plate. Unmold, garnish with additional chopped parsley, Parmesan, and diced tomatoes, and serve with Italian Tomato Sauce (page 160).

Shortcut Stacks

- You *can* use a prepackaged and preseasoned risotto. All you add is water. The taste will be fine—not as complex as making it from scratch, but easier and faster.

- Purchase a ready-made Italian tomato sauce.

Poached Salmon Timbale Stacks with Portobello Relish and Baby Greens

YIELD: 6 SERVINGS

This dish was an inspired by some wonderful leftover poached salmon. Since I have been preaching the convenience of making stacks with leftovers, I thought it best to follow my own advice. The result was terrific.

Planning Ahead

- Make more poached salmon than you need. This is a good "weekend guest" dish, because half the work is done with the poaching of the salmon.
- The relish can be made early in the day and set aside.
- The vinaigrette can be made 2 to 3 days in advance and refrigerated.
- Layer the stacks 2 to 3 hours ahead.
- Spoon dressing on at serving time.

SALMON

2 pounds fresh salmon fillets

1 cup white wine

$1^1/_2$ cups water

Zest of 1 lemon

1 bay leaf

1 teaspoon whole peppercorns

4 tablespoons basil oil (page 160)

4 tablespoons fresh basil, sliced into thin strips

2 tablespoons capers

$^1/_2$ cup peeled, seeded, and diced cucumber

1 avocado, peeled, pitted, and diced

1 tablespoon freshly squeezed lemon juice

1 tablespoon freshly squeezed lime juice

Salt and freshly ground black pepper to taste

PORTOBELLO RELISH

1 tablespoon butter

1 tablespoon extra virgin olive oil

1 pound portobello mushrooms, diced

$1^1/_2$ cups chopped whole green onions

$^1/_2$ cup julienned oil-packed sundried tomatoes, drained

2 cloves garlic, minced

$^1/_2$ cup mozzarella di bufala, diced

2 tablespoons chopped fresh basil

3 tablespoons balsamic vinegar

Salt and freshly ground black pepper to taste

6 cups baby greens

Honey-Lime Vinaigrette (recipe follows)

6 basil leaves, for garnish

Advance Preparation

To make the salmon, wrap the salmon in 2 layers of cheesecloth and tie at either end. Combine the wine, water, zest, and bay leaf in a large skillet. Bring to a boil. Add the salmon and immediately reduce the heat to simmer and poach for 8 minutes, or until the salmon is just cooked through and its center is opaque. When finished poaching, lift the salmon out of pan using the cheesecloth ends. Cut the cheesecloth off, drain the salmon, and allow it to cool to room temperature, about 20 minutes. Remove the skin and discard. Place salmon in a bowl and lightly flake with a fork. Gently stir in the remaining ingredients. Cover and set aside.

To make the relish, melt the butter and heat the oil in a large skillet. Add the mushrooms and sauté for 8 minutes. Add the onions, sundried tomatoes, and garlic and sauté 2 more minutes. Do not overcook. Remove from the heat, allow to cool, and stir in the remaining ingredients. Toss gently and chill.

Assembly

Spray 6 stack cylinders with vegetable spray and place them on a sheet pan. Layer in the following order: $1/2$ cup of salmon, packed; $1/4$ cup mushroom relish. Press gently but firmly to compact the layers. Chill for 1 hour.

To serve, slide a spatula under each stack cylinder and transfer to a serving plate. Unmold onto a bed of baby greens that have been tossed in vinaigrette, garnish with basil leaves, and serve.

Note: Try using a pyramid mold or a wider 5-inch-diameter ring mold for this dish.

This dish can be served heated if you wish. Place it in a 350° oven for 10 minutes before unmolding.

HONEY–LIME VINAIGRETTE
YIELD: $2/3$ CUP

2 teaspoons sweet and hot mustard

3 tablespoons Japanese seasoned rice wine vinegar

2 tablespoons freshly squeezed lime juice

1 tablespoon honey

$1/3$ cup canola oil

2 tablespoons minced fresh parsley

Combine the mustard, vinegar, lime juice, and honey and whisk until blended. Slowly add the canola oil, whisking until emulsified. Add the parsley and blend. Chill until needed.

Shortcut Stacks

• Purchase fresh poached salmon from a fish market or quality deli.

• Purchase a lime or lemon vinaigrette.

Grilled Prawn, Lemon Risotto, Asparagus, and Ginger Stacks with Mango-Watermelon Salsa

YIELD: 6 SERVINGS

This dish is summer entertaining at its best—easy to prepare and pretty. Serve it with a salad of baby greens.

Planning Ahead

- Prepare the asparagus the day before and chill.

- Prepare the salad 2 hours ahead and chill.

- When the risotto is almost completed, grill the prawns.

24 prawns, shelled and cleaned

3 tablespoons sesame oil

RISOTTO

4 to 5 cups chicken broth

1/2 cup freshly squeezed lemon juice

5 tablespoons butter

1 1/2 cups arborio rice

Zest of 1 lemon

3 tablespoons freshly grated Parmesan cheese

2 tablespoons minced fresh thyme

MANGO-WATERMELON SALSA

1 mango, peeled and diced

2 tablespoons chopped fresh cilantro

1/2 cup peeled and diced cucumber

1/4 cup peeled and diced jicama

1/2 cup diced watermelon

1 tablespoon freshly squeezed lime juice

Zest of 1/2 lemon

12 fresh asparagus spears, trimmed

6 tablespoons pickled ginger, chopped and drained

6 pieces pickled ginger, rolled into flowers, for garnish

Advance Preparation

To make the prawns, place the prawns on oiled skewers, brush lightly with sesame oil, and grill over hot coals for about 5 minutes. Then halve lengthwise and set aside. Or, place skewers under a high broiler flame and cook for 2 1/2 minutes per side.

To make the risotto, in a saucepan, heat the broth to a simmer. Heat the lemon juice, in a separate saucepan, to a simmer. Melt 3 tablespoons butter in a large saucepan. Stir in the rice to coat well. Adjust the heat to medium-high. Add 1 cup of hot broth to the rice and stir until the liquid is absorbed. Continue adding broth $1/2$ cup at a time, stirring and allowing liquid to be absorbed into the rice before the next addition. After 10 minutes add the lemon juice, stir until absorbed, and continue to add broth, stirring, as above. Total cooking time will be about 18 minutes. The rice should have a little bite to it and should not be mushy. Add the lemon zest, Parmesan, remaining butter, and thyme. Stir well. Keep warm.

To make the salsa, combine all of the salsa ingredients and chill, covered, in the refrigerator.

To make the asparagus, steam the spears for 4 minutes. Rinse in ice water, drain, and dice. Set aside.

Assembly

Preheat the oven to 350°.

Spray 6 stack cylinders with vegetable spray and place them on a sheet pan. Layer in the following order: 3 tablespoons risotto, 1 tablespoon asparagus, 4 halves of grilled prawns, 1 teaspoon chopped pickled ginger. Repeat the layers and top with a third layer of risotto. Press down gently but firmly. Bake for 10 minutes.

To serve, slide a spatula under each stack cylinder and transfer to a serving plate. Unmold, garnish with diced asparagus and a flower of pickled ginger, and serve immediately with salsa on the side.

Enchilada Stacks

SAVORY STACKS

Enchilada Stacks

YIELD: 6 SERVINGS

Everyone loves enchiladas. We've just put a new spin on an old favorite.

Planning Ahead

- Prepare the meat filling the day before and chill.
- Prepare the taco sauce 1 to 3 days in advance and chill, covered.
- Prep all of the garnish and place in bowls in the refrigerator, covered.

TORTILLAS

10 flour tortillas

4 tablespoons melted butter

FILLING

1 tablespoon vegetable oil

1 large onion, chopped

1$1/_2$ pounds ground beef or skinless, boneless chicken, diced

2 cloves garlic, minced

$3/_4$ cup green chile salsa

$1/_2$ cup Taco Sauce (recipe follows)

1 teaspoon choppped fresh oregano

Salt and freshly ground black pepper to taste

1 cup grated mozzarella cheese

1 cup grated Cheddar cheese

2 large tomatoes, seeded and diced

6 scallions, diced, for garnish

$2/_3$ cup fresh cilantro, chopped, for garnish

$1/_2$ cup sour cream, for garnish

1 avocado, diced, for garnish

Advance Preparation

To make the tortillas, using a 3$1/_2$-inch cutter, cut 3 rounds out of each tortilla and place on an oiled sheet pan. Brush each round lightly with melted butter and bake at 350° for 8 to 10 minutes, or until golden. Set aside. You will need 30 rounds. (The reason for a 3$1/_2$-inch cutter is that the tortillas shrink during cooking to 3 inches.)

To make the meat filling, heat the oil in a large skillet. Add the onion and sauté for 2 minutes. Add the beef and the garlic and sauté until beef is cooked through, about 10 minutes. Stir in the green chile salsa, the Taco Sauce, oregano, salt, and pepper. Decrease the heat and simmer for 20 to 30 minutes.

Assembly

Preheat the oven to 350°.

Spray 6 stack cylinders with vegetable spray and place them on a sheet pan. Layer the stacks in the following order: 1 tortilla round, 1 tablespoon meat filling, 1 tablespoon mixed mozzarella and Cheddar, $^1/_2$ tablespoon diced tomato. Repeat 3 more times and top with a fifth tortilla round. Press down firmly but gently. Bake for 10 minutes.

To serve, slide a spatula under each stack cylinder and transfer to a serving plate. Carefully unmold and garnish with scallions, cilantro, sour cream, avocado, and any leftover diced tomatoes and cheese. Pass additional Taco Sauce.

TACO SAUCE
YIELD: ABOUT 1$^1/_2$ CUPS

2 tablespoons vegetable oil

3 cloves garlic, minced

2 tablespoons all-purpose flour

2 tablespoons quality chile powder

1 (10-ounce) can chicken stock

Heat the oil in a medium saucepan. Add the garlic and sauté for 1 minute. Stir in the flour and blend. Stir in the chile powder. Bring the chicken stock to a simmer. Add the chicken stock while whisking, blending until the sauce is smooth and thickened. Reduce heat and simmer for 5 minutes.

Shortcut Stacks

- Buy a quality taco sauce.
- Buy ready-grated cheeses.

Warm Italian Chicken Salad with Wild Field Greens and Mustard-Honey Vinaigrette

YIELD: 6 SERVINGS

This is an elegant salad stack. I've placed it in this chapter because it really is a substantial meal, one that will wow your guests.

Planning Ahead

- Sauté the pancetta early and drain on paper towels.
- Prepare the chicken in the morning and chill. Reheat before serving.
- Make mushrooms and peppers in the morning. Chill. Reheat before serving.
- Make dressing the day before.
- Toast pine nuts ahead of time.

CHICKEN

1 cup diced pancetta

1 tablespoon extra virgin olive oil

3 whole (double) chicken breasts, skinned and boned

Salt and freshly ground black pepper to taste

1 teaspoon chopped fresh oregano

1 leek, white part only, rinsed well and chopped

2 shallots, chopped

3 cloves garlic, minced

3 cups portobello, shiitake, porcini, chanterelle, or oyster mushrooms, cleaned and stemmed

$1/2$ red bell pepper, chopped

$1/2$ cup white wine

2 tablespoons balsamic vinegar

1 teaspoon brown sugar

GREENS AND DRESSING

3 tablespoons seasoned rice wine vinegar

1 tablespoon freshly squeezed lemon juice

2 teaspoons honey

1 tablespoon sweet-hot mustard

$1/3$ cup extra virgin olive oil

Salt and freshly ground black pepper to taste

6 cups fresh field greens, washed, dried, and chilled

$1/2$ cup toasted pine nuts, for garnish (page 161)

Advance Preparation

To make the chicken and vegetables, sauté the pancetta in a large skillet over medium-high heat until crisp. Remove and drain on paper towels. In the same skillet, heat 1 tablespoon olive oil and sauté the chicken breasts until just cooked through, about 15 minutes. Season with salt, pepper, and oregano. Remove the chicken from the skillet and keep warm. Add the leek, shallots, and garlic to the skillet. Sauté until translucent, about 5 minutes. Remove from the skillet. Chop the chicken and combine with the leek mixture.

To the same skillet, add the mushrooms and red pepper and sauté until just cooked. Remove. Pour in the white wine and reduce by half. Then add the balsamic vinegar and sugar and cook, stirring, until the sauce becomes a glaze, about 5 minutes. Return the mushrooms and peppers to the skillet. Stir to coat with the glaze.

To make the dressing, combine the vinegar, lemon juice, honey, mustard, olive oil, salt, and pepper in a jar and shake to blend. Toss the greens lightly in 3 to 4 tablespoons of the dressing.

Assembly

Preheat oven to 350°.

Spray 6 stack cylinders with vegetable spray and place them on a sheet pan. Spoon $1/_2$ cup of chicken-leek mixture into each cylinder. Press down gently but firmly. Top chicken with 3 tablespoons mushroom mixture.

Bake for 10 minutes.

To serve, slide a spatula under each stack and transfer to a serving plate. Unmold, surround each stack with greens, and garnish stacks and greens with pancetta and pine nuts. Serve immediately.

Shortcut Stacks

Purchase a quality honey-mustard dressing.

Filet Mignon with Mushroom Ragout and Potato Tiles

YIELD: 6 SERVINGS

The inspiration for this dish came to me after I saw "potato tiles" at Harrods Food Hall in London. The result is a stunning dish, worthy of a great dinner party. Serve a big red wine with this!

Planning Ahead

- Make the potato tiles 2 hours before serving.
- Prepare the mushroom ragout the day before and chill. Reheat before serving.
- Prepare the horseradish cream the day before and chill.

POTATO TILES

6 extra-large russet potatoes, peeled

$1/2$ cup butter, melted

Salt and freshly ground black pepper to taste

$1/4$ teaspoon minced fresh thyme

$1/4$ teaspoon crumbled sage

FILETS MIGNONS

6 filets mignons, about 3 inches in diameter by 2 inches thick

6 slices prosciutto

Salt and freshly ground black pepper to taste

MUSHROOM RAGOUT

4 tablespoons butter

2 cups cleaned and chopped brown mushrooms

1 cup cleaned and chopped portobello mushrooms

1 cup cleaned and chopped shiitake mushrooms

2 cloves garlic, minced

1 leek, white part only, chopped

4 shallots, chopped

$1/4$ pound ground beef fillet trimmings

2 tablespoons chile sauce

2 tablespoons quality bottled steak sauce

1 teaspoon Worcestershire sauce

$3/4$ cup red wine

$1/4$ teaspoon minced fresh thyme

$1/4$ cup beef stock

1 teaspoon all-purpose flour

2 tablespoons heavy whipping cream

2 tablespoons chopped fresh parsley

Salt and freshly ground black pepper to taste

HORSERADISH CREAM

$1/2$ cup prepared horseradish

$1/4$ cup sour cream

3 tablespoons chives

3 tablespoons minced chives, for garnish

Advance Preparation

Preheat the oven to 375°.

To make the potato tiles, cut 3 of the potatoes into 18 $1/8$-inch-thick slices. Brush each slice with butter. Line a sheet pan with parchment paper and lay the buttered potato slices to cover the surface. Dust with salt, pepper, thyme, and sage. Bake for 10 minutes, or until cooked through and lightly browned. If the potatoes are small, prepare additional slices and overlap to make a 3-inch round.

Cut an additional 12 slices from the remaining potatoes, brush with butter and bake for 13 to 15 minutes, or until crisp and brown. Cut these crisp slices into triangles and set aside to use as garnish.

To make the filets, heat the grill to medium high. Wrap the circumference of each filet with a slice of prosciutto and secure with a length of twine. Season with salt and pepper. Do not cook the filets until 20 minutes before you assemble the stacks. Then grill the filets until the meat reaches a temperature of 150° (medium rare). Let rest 10 minutes.

To make the mushroom ragout, melt the butter in a large skillet and sauté the mushrooms for 10 minutes. Add the garlic, leek, and shallots and sauté 5 minutes. Add the ground fillet and brown. Add the chile sauce, steak sauce, Worcestershire, wine, thyme, beef stock, and flour and gently simmer for 30 minutes, stirring occasionally. Stir in the cream, parsley, salt, and pepper and keep warm.

To make the horseradish cream, mix together the horseradish, sour cream, and chives. Chill until serving time.

Assembly

Preheat the oven to 350°.

Place 6 potato tiles on a sheet pan. Cut the filets mignon in half, giving you twelve 3 by 1-inch rounds. Place 1 filet round on each potato tile. Top with a second potato tile and a second filet round. Top with a third potato tile. Spoon 3 tablespoons mushroom ragout on top of each stack and bake for 6 to 8 minutes.

To serve, spoon hot mushroom ragout on each of 6 serving plates. With a spatula, transfer the filet stacks to the plates, garnish with additional triangle tiles, horseradish cream, and chives, and serve immediately.

Sausage and Chicken Stacks with Grilled Onions and Peppers

YIELD: 6 SERVINGS

This dish has a Mediterranean flavor that pleases most tastes and is also very easy to make. Try using some of the gourmet sausages found in big supermarkets for a change of flavor.

Planning Ahead

- Grill the sausages and chicken ahead. Slice and chill. Bring to room temperature before stacking.

- Prepare the onions and peppers early in the day.

- Prepare the Tomato-Saffron Sauce the day before and chill. Warm before serving.

TIP: When grilling onions, to prevent slices from falling apart on the grill, run a thin metal skewer through the slice, to hold the layers together. Grill the onions on both sides. Remove skewers and serve.

4 small skinless, boneless chicken breasts

2 sweet Italian sausages

Salt and freshly ground black pepper to taste

3 tablespoons extra virgin olive oil

2 large onions, peeled and sliced $1/_3$ inch thick (see Tip)

1 red bell pepper, quartered and seeded

1 green bell pepper, quartered and seeded

1 cup orzo

$2/_3$ cup peas

1 cup Tomato-Saffron Sauce (recipe follows)

Advance Preparation

To make the chicken and sausages, season them lightly with salt and pepper, brush with 2 tablespoons olive oil, and grill or broil until cooked through and browned, about 15 minutes. Let cool 5 minutes. Chop the chicken coarsely and set aside. Slice the sausages and set aside.

Slice and skewer the onions. Brush the skewered onions with olive oil and grill until browned and cooked through. Chop and set aside.

Grill the peppers, skin side down, until the skin is blackened. Roll the blackened peppers in a paper towel and place them in a plastic bag to steam for 5 to 10 minutes. Remove the peppers, scrape the blackened skin off, discard the skin, and chop the peppers.

Cook the orzo in boiling water for 10 minutes and drain.

Cook the peas in boiling salted water for 3 minutes and drain.

Assembly

Preheat the oven to 375°.

Spray 6 stack cylinders with vegetable spray and place them on a sheet pan. Layer stacks in the following order: 2 tablespoons chicken, 2 tablespoons orzo, 2 tablespoons grilled onions, 2 tablespoons sliced sausage, $1^1/_2$ tablespoons grilled peppers, 1 tablespoon peas. Repeat layers and top with a third layer of chicken and orzo. Press down gently but firmly. Bake for 10 minutes. Let rest 3 minutes.

To serve, slide a spatula under each stack cylinder and transfer to a serving plate. Unmold and serve with Tomato-Saffron Sauce.

TOMATO-SAFFRON SAUCE
YIELD: ABOUT $1^1/_2$ CUPS

1 onion, diced

3 cloves garlic, minced

2 tablespoons extra virgin olive oil

5 ripe tomatoes, chopped

$^1/_4$ to $^1/_2$ teaspoon saffron, to taste

$^1/_2$ cup white wine

$^1/_2$ cup chicken stock, canned or homemade (page 161)

2 tablespoons chopped fresh parsley

1 teaspoon minced fresh thyme

$^1/_4$ teaspoon paprika

Salt and freshly ground black pepper to taste

Sauté the onion and garlic in olive oil over medium-high heat until soft. Add the tomatoes and sauté until they begin to release juice and soften. Add remaining ingredients and bring to a boil. Then immediately decrease heat to a simmer and cook for 1 hour, or until the sauce is thickened.

Beef Chili and Polenta Stacks

Kids love these. These stacks are familiar, comforting, and nutritious.

Planning Ahead

- Prepare the polenta rounds early in the day. (Wrap leftover polenta in plastic wrap and store in the refrigerator for another use. Try it sautéed in butter and served with Italian tomato sauce and Parmesan.)

- Make the chili the day before and chill. (This is not only convenient, it makes the chili taste better!)

- Prep the garnish and chill.

CHILI

$1^1/_2$ pounds lean ground beef or turkey

$1^1/_2$ onions, chopped

1 red bell pepper, chopped

3 cloves garlic, minced

1 tablespoon extra virgin olive oil

3 tablespoons chile powder

1 ($14^1/_2$-ounce) can diced tomatoes

2 fresh tomatoes, diced

1 ($14^1/_2$-ounce) can chili beans

$^1/_2$ teaspoon cumin

$^1/_8$ teaspoon cayenne, or more to taste

Dash of cinnamon

1 ear fresh corn, cleaned and kernels removed

POLENTA

1 ($13^1/_2$-ounce) package 5-minute polenta (page 164)

2 tablespoons butter

$^1/_2$ cup freshly grated Parmesan cheese

1 tablespoon chile powder

Salt and freshly ground black pepper to taste

8 whole green onions, chopped

1 cup grated Cheddar cheese, for garnish

6 tablespoons sour cream, for garnish

$^1/_2$ cup chopped cilantro, for garnish

Advance Preparation

To make the chili, brown the beef, onions, pepper, and garlic in 1 tablespoon oil in a large saucepan or Dutch oven. Add the chile powder and tomatoes and cook 1 minute. Add the beans, cumin, cayenne, cinnamon, and corn and simmer for 1 hour, adding a little water if the chili becomes too dry. (It should not be watery, however.)

To make the polenta, prepare the polenta according to the directions on page 164, stirring in the butter, Parmesan, chile powder, salt, and pepper near the end of the preparation. Pour the polenta into a lightly greased 12 by 17-inch sheet pan and smooth to a $1/_2$-inch depth. Let rest 20 minutes to firm up. With a stack cylinder or 3-inch cutter, cut the polenta into rounds. You will need 18 rounds.

Assembly

Preheat the oven to 350°.

Spray 6 stack cylinders with vegetable spray and place them on a sheet pan. Layer in the following order: 1 polenta round, 3 tablespoons chili, 2 tablespoons cheese, 1 tablespoon green onions. Repeat layers and top with a third polenta round. Press down gently but firmly and bake for 10 minutes. Remove and let rest 2 minutes.

To serve, slide a spatula under each stack and transfer to a serving plate. Unmold and garnish with cheese, sour cream, cilantro, and any remaining green onions. Pass additional chili, if desired.

Shortcut Stacks

- Purchase a quality chili or go to your local gourmet-to-go and purchase chili freshly made.

- Use the ready-made polenta found in your deli case. It comes in 3-inch tubes and can be sliced.

Zucchini and Bulgur Stacks with Grilled Chicken

YIELD: 6 SERVINGS

A nod to healthful stack presentations, this can also be a side stack by eliminating the chicken. Try it with big, fat Parmesan curls.

Planning Ahead

- Prepare the bulgur early in the day.
- Prepare the zucchini 1 to 2 hours early.
- Grill the chicken prior to stacking.
- Stacks can be assembled and chilled 1 to 2 hours before baking. Bring to room temperature before baking.

BULGUR

1 large leek, diced, white and palest green part only

1 large portobello mushroom, chopped

2 large brown mushrooms, chopped

2 tablespoons butter

1 cup bulgur

2 cups chicken stock (page 161)

1 teaspoon minced fresh oregano

$1/_2$ teaspoon minced fresh thyme

Salt and freshly ground black pepper to taste

ZUCCHINI

$1/_3$ pound pancetta, diced

1 large onion, peeled and chopped

4 cloves garlic

4 zucchini, chopped

Freshly ground black pepper to taste

3 tomatoes, seeded and diced

4 tablespoons chopped Italian parsley

2 tablespoons grated Parmesan cheese

CHICKEN

2 whole (double) skinless, boneless chicken breasts

2 tablespoons extra virgin olive oil

Salt and freshly ground black pepper to taste

Italian Tomato Sauce (page 160)

TIP: To make Parmesan curls, run a vegetable peeler along the length of a room-temperature block of quality Parmesan cheese.

Advance Preparation

Preheat oven to 350°.

To make the bulgur, in a large ovenproof saucepan, sauté the leek and mushrooms in butter until limp, about 5 minutes. Add the bulgur and cook, stirring, 1 minute. Add the stock, oregano, thyme, salt, and pepper. Bring to a boil, stirring. Cover and bake at 350° for 20 minutes. Fluff with a fork.

To make the zucchini, sauté the diced pancetta in a large skillet for 2 to 3 minutes. Add the onion and garlic and sauté 5 minutes over medium heat. Do not allow the garlic to burn. Add the zucchini and pepper and cook for 10 to 15 minutes, or until the zucchini is tender and just cooked through. Add the tomatoes, parsley, and Parmesan. Set aside.

To make the chicken, brush the breasts with oil, season with salt and pepper, and grill over medium-hot coals or on a gas grill until golden and cooked through, 15 to 20 minutes. Let rest 5 minutes and then dice the chicken. Set aside.

Assembly

Preheat the oven to 350°.

Spray 6 stack cylinders and place them on a sheet pan. Layer the stacks in the following order: 2 tablespoons diced chicken, 2 tablespoons bulgur, 2 tablespoons zucchini mixture. Repeat the layers and top with any leftover chicken. Press down gently but firmly. Bake for 10 minutes or until hot.

To serve, slide a spatula under each stack cylinder and transfer to a serving plate. Serve with Italian Tomato Sauce or diced fresh tomatoes sautéed for 2 minutes over high heat with a little olive oil, garlic, and chopped Italian parsley.

Grilled Chicken and Couscous Stacks with Parmesan Cookies

YIELD: 6 SERVINGS

I love this dish! The flavors are Mediterranean and the Parmesan cookies give it a sense of fun. When making the cookies, try to mold them into fun shapes while they are still warm.

Planning Ahead

- Grill the chicken and vegetables early in the day and chill.

- Prepare the couscous 1 hour before stacking.

- Prepare the tomatoes the day before and chill. They can be reheated before serving.

- Prepare the Parmesan cookies 1 to 2 hours before serving. (They can be prepared ahead—the day before—and stored in an airtight container; however, the taste is better when fresh. If the cookies become soft, heat them for 2 to 3 minutes in a 350° oven.)

TIP: To avoid a mess on the counter when grating Parmesan, wrap a plastic baggy around the bottom of the grater and secure with a rubber band. Grate the cheese onto the plastic and avoid messy cleanup.

CHICKEN AND VEGETABLES

2 whole (double) chicken breasts, boned (remove the skin for reduced fat)

6 zucchini, trimmed and sliced lengthwise $1/4$ inch thick

1 eggplant, cut into 12 $1/4$-inch slices

3 tablespoons extra virgin olive oil

Salt and freshly ground pepper to taste

COUSCOUS

$1/3$ cup currants

2 cups water

$1 1/2$ tablespoons extra virgin olive oil

$1 1/2$ cups couscous

$1/2$ teaspoon salt

Freshly ground pepper to taste

$1/2$ teaspoon curry powder

$1/2$ teaspoon minced fresh oregano

$1/3$ cup toasted pine nuts (page 161)

SAUCE

10 tomatoes, cut into chunks

3 tablespoons extra virgin olive oil

Salt and freshly ground black pepper
  to taste

4 cloves garlic, minced

6 whole green onions, chopped

$1/2$ cup white wine

1 tablespoon minced fresh oregano

$1/4$ cup chopped fresh parsley

PARMESAN COOKIES

$1^1/2$ cups freshly grated Parmesan cheese

$1/3$ teaspoon curry powder

3 tablespoons very fine cake flour

Advance Preparation

First, soak the currants in hot water for 30 minutes.

To make the chicken and vegetables, lightly brush the chicken and vegetables with olive oil. Salt and pepper to taste. To grill, place the chicken and vegetables over hot coals and grill until browned and cooked through. The chicken will take about 20 minutes, the vegetables about 10 minutes. Chop the cooked chicken and zucchini. Trim the eggplant slices into 3-inch rounds. Set aside.

To make the couscous, drain the currants that have been soaking in hot water. Set aside. Bring the water and olive oil to a boil. Add the couscous, bring back to a boil, cover, and remove from heat. Let stand 5 minutes and fluff with a fork. Stir in the salt, pepper, curry, oregano, pine nuts, and currants. Fluff again. Set aside.

To make the tomato sauce, brush the tomatoes with 2 tablespoons olive oil and place in a large sheet pan, cut side up. Salt and pepper to taste. Roast at 300° for 2 hours, or until soft.

Heat 1 tablespoon olive oil in a large saucepan. Sauté the garlic until soft. Add the onions and sauté 1 minute. Add the roasted tomatoes and cook for 5 minutes. Add the wine, oregano, parsley, salt, and pepper. Simmer gently until thickened and the flavors have blended, about 30 minutes.

To make the Parmesan cookies, mix together the Parmesan, curry, and flour. Heat a small, nonstick skillet over a medium-high flame. Sprinkle $2^1/_2$ tablespoons Parmesan mixture evenly over the bottom surface of the skillet and, using a metal spatula, "tidy up" the edges. When the cookie is lightly browned, carefully turn it and brown the other side. When turning, flip the cookie quickly. Don't be tentative, as the cookies tend to be soft and will stick. If the first 2 or 3 don't work, keep trying. It becomes easier. These are much like crepes. Place the cookies on a plate to cool, or drape over a rolling pin or bottle to give them a curve.

Assembly

Preheat the oven to 350°.

Spray 6 stack cylinders with vegetable spray and place them on a sheet pan. Layer in the following order: 3 tablespoons couscous, 1 slice eggplant, 2 tablespoons chicken-zucchini. Repeat the layers and top with a third layer of couscous. Press down gently but firmly. Bake for 10 minutes.

To serve, slide a spatula under each stack cylinder and transfer to a serving plate. Unmold, spoon tomato sauce around the base, and garnish with Parmesan cookies.

Shortcut Stacks

- Purchase a quality tomato pasta sauce.
- Use packaged flavored couscous mix (Mediterranean or Italian flavor).

Duck with Cannellini Beans, Tomato, Pancetta, and Mediterranean Compote

A wonderful winter dish for company, this host's or hostess's dream can be made a day before serving. Make sure the duck breast is of the best quality you can get from your butcher.

Planning Ahead

- Marinate the duck the day before.
- Prepare the beans the day before and reheat prior to stacking.
- Prepare the Mediterranean compote the day before and reheat prior to serving.

1 whole duck breast, boned

MARINADE

$^1/_2$ cup red wine

$^1/_4$ cup extra virgin olive oil

3 cloves garlic, minced

1 teaspoon Dijon mustard

$^1/_4$ cup chopped fresh rosemary

1 teaspoon salt

Freshly ground black pepper to taste

BEANS

1 pound cannellini beans

2 tablespoons extra virgin olive oil

1 large onion, chopped

4 large cloves garlic, minced

1 teaspoon *herbes de Provence*

1 tablespoon chopped fresh rosemary

1 teaspoon salt

Freshly ground black pepper to taste

1 ($14^1/_2$-ounce) can diced tomatoes

4 zucchini, quartered lengthwise, then chopped

1 teaspoon extra virgin olive oil

6 slices pancetta, diced

$2^1/_2$ cups Mediterranean Compote (recipe follows)

Advance Preparation

To make the duck, combine the marinade ingredients and mix well. Place the marinade and duck in a large plastic bag and marinate several hours, or overnight. Drain the duck and grill until just cooked through, about 15 minutes. Let rest 10 minutes, then slice into $^1/_2$-inch pieces. Set aside.

To make the beans, boil the beans for 1 hour, then drain. Heat the olive oil in a large Dutch oven and sauté the onion and garlic until soft. Add the beans, herbs, salt, pepper, and enough water to cover. Bring to a boil, reduce the heat, and simmer for an hour. Check for doneness. The beans should be soft but they should still hold their shape. Drain off excess liquid, add tomatoes, and cook another 30 minutes, or until beans are cooked and thickened somewhat. Bean mixture should be fairly thick. If not, cook a little longer or drain off some liquid. Set aside.

To make the zucchini, sauté the zucchini in the olive oil for 3 minutes. Set aside.

Place the pancetta in a small skillet over medium-high heat and sauté, stirring occasionally, until crisp, about 10 minutes. Drain on paper towels and set aside.

Assembly

Preheat the oven to 375°.

Spray 6 stack cylinders with vegetable spray and place them on a sheet pan. Layer the stacks in the following order: 3 tablespoons duck, 3 tablespoons beans, 1 tablespoon pancetta, $1^1/_2$ tablespoons zucchini. Repeat the layers. Press down gently but firmly. Bake for 10 minutes. Remove and let rest 5 minutes.

To serve, slide a spatula under each stack cylinder and transfer to a serving plate. Unmold and serve with Mediterranean Compote on the side.

Shortcut Stacks

- Purchase a precooked duck, remove the meat, and slice it into small pieces.
- Use canned, drained cannellini beans instead of dried beans. Add to the onion, garlic, and herbs, cook 10 minutes, and add the tomatoes.

MEDITERRANEAN COMPOTE
YIELD: ABOUT $2^1/_2$ CUPS

1 bulb fennel, trimmed and cut into 8 pieces

2 onions, peeled and cut into 8 pieces

6 cloves garlic, peeled

8 Roma tomatoes, quartered

Salt and freshly ground black pepper to taste

$1/_4$ teaspoon fennel seeds

3 tablespoons extra virgin olive oil

$1/_2$ cup halved and pitted niçoise olives

3 tablespoons chopped fresh parsley

Place the fennel, onions, garlic, and tomatoes in a deep baking pan. Season with salt, pepper, and fennel seeds and pour olive oil over the vegetables. Bake at 375° for 30 minutes. Cover and continue to bake at 325° for 1 hour, or until vegetables are very tender. Stir in the olives and parsley.

Note: This is also delicious served over pasta with a generous sprinkling of freshly grated Parmesan cheese.

Grilled Lamb, Caramelized Onion, and Spinach Stacks with Garlic Mashed Potatoes and Stilton

YIELD: 6 SERVINGS

Anything with garlic mashed potatoes is my favorite. It reminds me of meat loaf and mashed potatoes when I was a little girl. My mom made a mean meat loaf and perfectly yummy mashed potatoes. (This stack is also great for leftover lamb roast.)

Planning Ahead

- Plan on serving a lamb roast 1 to 2 days ahead and use the leftover lamb for stacks.

- Prepare the stacks 3 hours ahead and chill. Bring to room temperature before baking.

MASHED POTATOES

2 large russet potatoes, peeled and cut into large chunks

3 cloves garlic

2 tablespoons butter

1 teaspoon minced fresh thyme

$1/2$ teaspoon salt

Freshly ground pepper to taste

$1/4$ cup half-and-half

ONIONS

4 large onions, sliced

2 tablespoons butter

$1/4$ cup chicken stock (page 161)

2 tablespoons brown sugar

2 teaspoons Worcestershire sauce

2 teaspoons balsamic vinegar

1 lamb loin

1 tablespoon olive oil

SPINACH

3 large bunches fresh spinach, washed, stemmed, and dried

2 tablespoons butter

2 cloves garlic

Salt and freshly ground black pepper to taste

Dash of nutmeg

1 cup peeled and diced carrots

$3/4$ cup crumbled Stilton cheese

3 tablespoons toasted walnuts (page 161)

Advance Preparation

To make the potatoes, boil the potatoes in salted water to cover for 20 minutes, or until tender. Drain. Gently sauté the garlic in the butter for 5 minutes. Mash the potatoes, add the garlic butter, thyme, salt, and pepper. Whip in the half-and half a little at a time. Potatoes should be smooth and creamy but be able to hold their shape. Set aside.

To make the onions, in a large skillet sauté the onions in the butter until very soft. Add the stock and brown sugar and cook over medium heat until onions are rich and caramelized, stirring often. Stir in the Worcestershire and vinegar. Set aside.

To make the lamb, lightly oil the lamb loin with the olive oil. Place over hot coals and grill for about 15 minutes, or until medium rare in the center. Remove, let stand 5 minutes, and coarsely chop. Set aside.

To make the spinach, steam the spinach in a large pot with whatever water remains on the leaves after rinsing. When wilted, drain very well and squeeze out any excess moisture. Chop the spinach and quickly sauté with butter and garlic. Season with salt, pepper, and nutmeg. Set aside.

To make the carrots, cook the carrots in boiling salted water until just tender, about 4 minutes.

Assembly

Preheat the oven to 350°.

Spray 6 stack cylinders with vegetable spray and place them on a sheet pan. Layer in the following order: 2 tablespoons garlic mashed potatoes, 1 tablespoon spinach, 2 to 3 tablespoons of lamb, 1 tablespoon caramelized onions, 1 tablespoon Stilton, 1 tablespoon carrots. Repeat and top with a third layer of mashed potatoes. Sprinkle with any leftover Stilton and bake for 10 minutes, or until heated through.

To serve, slide a spatula under each stack cylinder and transfer to a serving plate. Unmold, garnish with chopped walnuts and additional onions, and serve.

Grilled Duck Stacks with Honey–Shallot–Ginger Sauce

YIELD: 6 SERVINGS

I love the combination of duck, cabbage, and sweet potatoes, so decided to try it in a stack. These remind me of comfort food and are perfect for dinner with friends, served with a big red wine.

Planning Ahead

- Assemble the stacks in the late afternoon and chill. Bring to room temperature prior to baking.

- Make the sauce 1 to 3 hours ahead. Pour very hot sauce into a thermos bottle and seal. (Or you may make the sauce early in the day, chill, and reheat prior to serving.)

DUCK

1 whole duck breast, boned (see Note)

1/2 teaspoon freshly ground black pepper

1/2 teaspoon freshly ground nutmeg

1/2 teaspoon powdered ginger

1 tablespoon extra virgin olive oil

CABBAGE

4 tablespoons butter

6 shallots, chopped

1 head red cabbage, shredded

2 tablespoons balsamic vinegar

4 green apples, peeled, cored, and chopped

1/2 cup brown sugar

1 teaspoon cinnamon

1/2 teaspoon cardamom

1/4 teaspoon cloves

1/2 cup red wine

5 tablespoons brandy

3 tablespoons dried cherries

Zest of 1 orange

4 sweet potatoes

3 large green apples, seeds removed, sliced into 1/4-inch rounds

2 tablespoons melted butter

1 cup Honey–Shallot–Ginger Sauce (recipe follows)

3 tablespoons minced fresh parsley, for garnish

3 tablespoons diced apple, for garnish

Advance Preparation

To grill the duck breast, rub it generously with the spices. Prick skin with a fork. Brush the duck with a little olive oil and grill for a total of 10 to 12 minutes, or until just cooked through. Transfer to a warm plate, cover, and let stand 5 minutes. Cut the duck meat into a 1/2-inch dice. Set aside.

To cook the cabbage, preheat the oven to 350°. Melt the butter in a large saucepan and sauté the shallots until softened. Add the cabbage and sauté for 5 minutes. Add the vinegar, apples, sugar, cinnamon, cardamom, and cloves and simmer for 15 minutes. Stir in the red wine, brandy, dried cherries, and orange zest. Cover and bake at 350° for $1^1/_2$ hours.

To make the sweet potatoes, bake them for 45 minutes at 350°, or until tender. Remove pulp and mash coarsely. Set aside.

To grill the apples, brush the apple slices with melted butter. Grill or broil for about 5 minutes, or until apples are cooked through but not mushy. Set aside.

Assembly

Preheat the oven to 350°.

Spray 6 stack cylinders with vegetable spray and place them on a sheet pan. Layer as follows: 1 grilled apple slice, 3 tablespoons mashed sweet potato, 2 tablespoons diced duck, 2 tablespoons cooked cabbage and apples. Repeat the layers. Press down gently but firmly. Bake stacks for 10 minutes, or until heated through.

To serve, slide a spatula under each stack and transfer to a serving plate. Spoon Honey-Shallot-Ginger Sauce around the base of the stack, unmold, and serve immediately. Garnish with chopped parsley and diced fresh apple, if desired.

Note: Duck breast is now available in many markets. Look for Muscovy boneless duck breast. In a hurry? Go to your local Chinatown, Chinese restaurant, or gourmet-to-go store and buy a cooked duck.

This stack is particularly good for leftover turkey, goose, chicken, or roast pork and is a great holiday dish. It can be made ahead, refrigerated, and warmed just before serving. Easy and elegant!

HONEY-SHALLOT-GINGER SAUCE
YIELD: $1^1/_2$ CUPS

This sauce is also great served with roast pork, ham, or grilled turkey.

2 tablespoons chopped shallots

1 tablespoon butter

$^1/_4$ cup duck stock or rich chicken stock (page 161)

$^1/_4$ cup dry white wine

1 teaspoon powdered ginger

1 teaspoon cardamom

1 cup heavy whipping cream

2 tablespoons Dijon mustard

2 teaspoons honey

Sauté shallots in butter. Add the stock, wine, ginger, and cardamom. Reduce for 10 minutes over medium heat, stirring often. Add the cream and simmer for 10 minutes. Add the mustard and honey. Whisk to blend.

Shortcut Stacks

Purchase a prepared duck (or duck breast) from a good gourmet-to-go or Chinese restaurant.

Beef Burger Stacks

YIELD: 6 SERVINGS

These free-form stacks look more involved than they really are. Almost everything can be made ahead and ready for the final stacking. They are fun to serve.

Planning Ahead

- Stuff the beef patties and chill.
- Roast the tomatoes the day before and chill.
- Make the sweet potato chips early in the day.
- Sauté the mushrooms 1 hour prior to serving.
- Have the washed and dried watercress and the buns ready.
- At serving time, grill the meat patties and sauté the onions.

BEEF BURGERS

2 pounds ground sirloin beef

6 tablespoons blue cheese

1 teaspoon minced fresh thyme

Salt and freshly ground black pepper to taste

6 slices herbed Brie

ROASTED TOMATOES

6 tomatoes, sliced into $1/4$-inch-thick rounds

2 tablespoons chopped fresh rosemary

Salt and freshly ground black pepper to taste

3 tablespoons extra virgin olive oil

MUSHROOMS

3 large portobello mushrooms

2 tablespoons butter

Salt and freshly ground black pepper to taste

SWEET POTATO CHIPS

3 sweet potatoes, peeled and sliced very thin

4 cups vegetable oil for frying, or enough to submerge the sweet potatoes in while frying

2 teaspoons sea salt

SPICY TOBACCO ONIONS

2 onions, sliced paper thin

2 cups cake flour

1 tablespoon cayenne pepper

4 cups vegetable oil for frying

2 teaspoons sea salt

6 best-quality hamburger buns, split

2 bunches watercress, washed, trimmed, and dried

6 tablespoons sweet and hot mustard

Advance Preparation

To make the burgers, divide the beef into 6 even patties. Bury 1 tablespoon of blue cheese (a solid piece not crumbled) into the center of each burger, enclosing it completely. Reshape patties and sprinkle with thyme, salt, and pepper.

To make the roasted tomatoes, place the tomatoes in a single layer on a large 12 by 17-inch sheet pan. Sprinkle with rosemary, salt, and pepper. Drizzle with oil and bake at 300° for 3 hours, or until the tomatoes are almost dried but still have some moisture. Set aside.

To make the mushrooms, slice the mushrooms and sauté in butter until rich and glossy looking. Season with salt and pepper. Keep warm.

To make the sweet potato chips, heat the oil to 425°. Fry the potato slices until lightly browned and crisp. Drain on paper towels and sprinkle with sea salt. Set aside.

To make the tobacco onions, heat the oil to 425°. Just before frying, dredge the onions in the flour and cayenne that have been mixed together. Shake well to remove excess flour. Fry until golden brown, drain, sprinkle with sea salt, and set aside.

Assembly

Ten minutes before serving, grill or pan-fry the patties until brown and cooked through, about 10 minutes. Place a slice of herbed Brie on top of each hot patty and allow to melt. Toast or grill the buns and spread generously with mustard. Divide watercress into 6 portions and place on the bottom buns. Layer in the following order: 1 beef burger patty, 3 slices roasted tomatoes, 3 slices sautéed mushrooms, 4 to 5 sweet potato chips, a generous dollop of tobacco onions.

Serve immediately with tops of buns leaning against the stack.

Shortcut Stacks

- Purchase sweet potato chips.
- Substitute sundried tomatoes for roasted tomatoes.

Italian Chicken Stacks

YIELD: 6 SERVINGS

When making stacks with pasta, make sure you allow the resting period after baking. This allows the hot pasta to cool enough to allow the gluten to activate, holding the stack together.

Planning Ahead

- These stacks do very well when made several hours ahead and chilled. Bring to room temperature before baking.

- Make tomatoes the day before.

- Make pesto the day before.

- Toast pine nuts as much as a week ahead and freeze. (I make large quantities of toasted nuts and store them in resealable plastic bags in the freezer.)

2 to 3 whole (double) skinless, boneless chicken breasts

TOMATOES

6 tomatoes, diced

1 yellow bell pepper, diced

2 bunches fresh basil, diced

4 cloves garlic, minced

10 whole green onions, chopped

$1/3$ cup extra virgin olive oil

$1/2$ teaspoon salt

$1/4$ teaspoon freshly ground black pepper

1 (16-ounce) package angel hair pasta

$3/4$ cup ricotta cheese

$1/2$ cup pesto (page 160)

$1/2$ cup freshly grated Parmesan cheese

$1/3$ cup toasted pine nuts (page 161)

Advance Preparation

Place the chicken breasts over hot coals and grill, turning once, for about 20 minutes, or until the center is no longer pink. Remove from the grill, let stand 5 minutes, then coarsely chop. Set aside.

To make the tomatoes, combine the tomatoes, bell pepper, basil, garlic, onions, olive oil, salt, and pepper. Let stand at room temperature for 1 to 2 hours. Just prior to assembling the stacks, very quickly sauté the tomato mixture over high heat for 3 minutes.

To make the pasta, prepare according to the package directions and drain.

Assembly

Preheat the oven to 350°.

Spray 6 stack cylinders with vegetable spray and place them on a sheet pan. Layer in the following order: 3 tablespoons pasta, 2 tablespoons tomatoes, 2 tablespoons chicken, 1 tablespoon ricotta, 1 teaspoon pesto, 1 tablespoon Parmesan, 1 teaspoon pine nuts. Repeat and top with a third layer of pasta. Press down gently but firmly. Bake for 10 minutes. Let stand 3 minutes.

To serve, slide a spatula under each stack cylinder and transfer to a serving plate. Unmold, garnish with any remaining tomatoes, pine nuts, and Parmesan, and serve.

Shortcut Stacks

- Purchase a quality pesto.
- Purchase a precooked chicken at your local deli or gourmet-to-go.
- Purchase a quality tomato pasta sauce.
- Have the Parmesan pregrated at your deli.

Pumpkin Risotto Stacks

A terrific change of pace for holiday entertaining—try these stacks with roasted turkey, goose, or capons. If pumpkin is out of season, try using a hard yellow squash such as Hubbard, Carnival, Golden Nugget, or Table Queen.

TIP: To skim turkey, chicken, or beef fat off the surface of a hot roasting pan, stir 1 or more cups of ice into the hot drippings. The hot fat will cling to the frozen cubes. Remove the cubes as they become coated with fat and discard. All that remains will be fat-free drippings.

Planning Ahead

- Prepare the candied pecans 1 to 3 days ahead and store in an airtight container.
- Prepare and assemble the stacks early in the day and chill. Bake just prior to serving.

RISOTTO

5 cups chicken stock (page 161)

2 tablespoons sweet butter

$1/2$ onion, chopped

2 shallots, chopped

$2/3$ cup grated fresh pumpkin

$1 1/2$ cups arborio rice

$1/4$ teaspoon freshly ground nutmeg

$1/4$ teaspoon ginger

$2/3$ cup grated Gruyère cheese

$1/2$ cup Candied Pecans (recipe follows)

$1/2$ cup dried cranberries

Advance Preparation

To make the risotto, heat the chicken stock to a simmer. Melt 2 tablespoons butter in a large saucepan and sauté the onion and shallots until limp. Add the pumpkin and sauté for 2 minutes. Add the rice and stir to coat with the butter. Pour $1/2$ cup simmering chicken stock into the rice. Adjust the heat to medium-high, so the rice is bubbling gently. Stir until the stock is absorbed, about 2 minutes. Continue adding stock $1/2$ cup at a time, stirring until it is absorbed before adding more. Cook the risotto, adding stock as needed, for 18 minutes. Remove the pan from the heat and stir in the nutmeg, ginger, and 4 tablespoons Gruyère cheese.

Assembly

Preheat the oven to 350°.

Spray 6 stack cylinders with vegetable spray and place them on a sheet pan. Layer in the following order: 3 tablespoons rice, 1 tablespoon Candied Pecans, 3 tablespoons rice, 1 tablespoon cranberries, 3 tablespoons rice. Sprinkle each top with 1 tablespoon Gruyère cheese. Bake for 5 to 8 minutes, or until the stacks are heated through and the cheese is bubbling.

To serve, slide a spatula under each stack cylinder and transfer to a serving plate. Unmold, garnish with additional chopped Candied Pecans, and serve immediately.

CANDIED PECANS
YIELD: 4 CUPS

This also makes a great hostess gift for the holidays.

1 pound shelled pecan halves

2 cups brown sugar

$1/_2$ cup milk

1 tablespoon white vinegar

Place the pecans in an even layer on a sheet pan. In a heavy saucepan, bring the sugar and milk to a boil over medium-high heat, stirring. Watch carefully so the pot does not boil over. Add the vinegar and continue to boil until the syrup reaches 230° on a candy thermometer, or forms a soft ball when a little is tested by dropping it into ice water. Pour the syrup over the nuts, coating them evenly. Allow to cool to room temperature. Separate the nuts.

Shortcut Stacks

Purchase candied pecans.

Caramelized Pear and Gingerbread Stacks

SWEET STACKS

Caramelized Pear and Gingerbread Stacks

YIELD: 6 SERVINGS

This is a beautiful fall dessert. The flavors of gingerbread, pears, and cinnamon conjure up memories of my childhood—gingerbread cookies and pear butter, yum!

Planning Ahead

- Make the gingerbread up to a week early. Wrap well in plastic wrap and freeze. Thaw before cutting out rounds.

- Make the cinnamon cream 1 to 2 days early. Cover and chill.

- Assemble several hours ahead and chill.

GINGERBREAD

2 cups apple sauce

1 cup dark molasses

3 cups cake flour, sifted

1 teaspoon baking powder

$1/_2$ teaspoon salt

$1/_2$ teaspoon ground star anise (see Note)

$1 1/_2$ teaspoons confectioners' sugar

$1/_2$ teaspoon ground cardamom

2 teaspoons ground cinnamon

$1/_2$ teaspoon ground cloves

4 large eggs, separated

1 cup sugar

$1/_2$ cup brown sugar

$2/_3$ cup vegetable oil

PEARS

$1/_2$ cup chopped macadamia nuts

3 tablespoons dried cherries

1 tablespoon flour

$1/_4$ teaspoon cinnamon

$1/_8$ teaspoon freshly ground nutmeg

Pinch of salt

$1/_2$ cup butter

$1 1/_4$ cups sugar

$2 1/_2$ pounds pears, peeled, cored, and cut into 8 pieces lengthwise

CINNAMON CREAM

1 cup mascarpone or cream cheese

2 tablespoons brown sugar

1 teaspoon ground cinnamon

$1/_2$ teaspoon freshly ground nutmeg

$1/_2$ teaspoon vanilla

$1/_2$ cup chopped macadamia nuts

Advance Preparation

Preheat the oven to 350°.

Grease a 12 by 17-inch sheet pan and line with parchment. Mix together the apple sauce and molasses in a medium saucepan and bring to a boil. Remove from the heat and cool slightly.

Sift together the flour with the baking powder, salt, star anise, confectioners' sugar, cardamom, cinnamon, and cloves. Set aside.

In a large bowl, beat the egg yolks until thick and lemony. Beat in the sugar and brown sugar and gradually beat in the oil. In a separate bowl, beat the egg whites until stiff. Add the warm applesauce-molasses mixture to the egg yolk mixture, then stir in the flour until smooth. Fold in the egg whites. Pour into the prepared sheet pan, smooth, and bake for 25 minutes, or until golden and slightly pulling away from the pan sides. Cool 5 minutes, then invert onto a rack and cool completely.

To make the pears, preheat the oven to 400°.

Combine the macadamia nuts, dried cherries, flour, cinnamon, nutmeg, and salt in a bowl. In a heavy 10-inch ovenproof skillet, melt the butter and sugar. Bring to a boil and cook until caramelized. Place the pears in the skillet, rounded side down, and cook over medium heat, basting, until coated with caramel. Sprinkle the pears with the macadamia mixture and bake uncovered in the oven for 5 minutes. Reserve the remaining sauce in the skillet.

To make the cinnamon cream, combine all the ingredients and blend well. Refrigerate until needed.

Assembly

Spray 6 stack cylinders with vegetable spray and place them on a sheet pan. Cut the gingerbread into 18 3-inch rounds. (Reserve the remaining cake for another use.) Frost each round with 1 tablespoon cinnamon cream. Separate the pears from the caramel sauce and chop half of the pears coarsely. Reserve the remaining pears. Layer in the following order: 1 frosted gingerbread round, 2 tablespoons chopped pears, 1 teaspoon macadamia nuts, 1 tablespoon caramel sauce (from skillet). Repeat and top with a third gingerbread round. Press down gently but firmly and chill for 2 hours or longer.

To serve, slide a spatula under each stack and transfer to a serving plate. Unmold, garnish the top of the stacks with the remaining pear slices, sprinkle with macadamia nuts, and drizzle caramel sauce over all. Spoon 1 to 2 tablespoons cinnamon cream at the base of each stack and serve.

Note: These stacks can be made several hours ahead. To warm, bring to room temperature, preheat the oven to 350°, and bake stacks for about 5 minutes. Unmold and serve.

Star anise is available in gourmet groceries or by mail from Bristol Farms (page 170). You can grind it in a small coffee grinder for about 15 seconds.

Shortcut Stacks

- Purchase an unfrosted gingerbread sheet cake from a quality bakery.

Summer Berry Charlotte Stacks

YIELD: 6 SERVINGS

A charlotte is a mold lined with cake, bread, or ladyfingers, then filled with a mousse, pudding, or fruit mixture. It is then chilled for several hours and unmolded onto a serving plate and garnished. The color of this dessert will amaze you. It comes out this rich deep, purply red, and the taste is truly the essence of lazy summer days.

Planning Ahead

Good news! You *have* to make this 24 hours in advance! Need I say more! A perfect entertaining recipe that'll knock their socks off.

24 slices good-quality day-old white sandwich bread, crusts removed

BERRIES

10 ounces fresh blueberries, washed and picked over

8 ounces fresh blackberries, washed and picked over

12 ounces fresh raspberries, washed and picked over

8 ounces fresh strawberries, washed, stemmed, and quartered

$3/4$ cup sugar

LEMON CRÈME FRAÎCHE

1 cup crème fraîche

$1^1/_2$ teaspoons freshly squeezed lemon juice

1 tablespoon grated lemon zest

1 tablespoon sugar

$1^1/_2$ cups additional fresh berries, for garnish

Advance Preparation

To make the berries, place all the ingredients for berries into a heavy saucepan. Bring to a boil, lower heat to a simmer, and cook for 3 minutes, or until the berries give up a rich, purply juice. Remove from the heat and allow the berries to cool slightly.

To make the crème fraîche, whisk together all ingredients and chill until serving time.

Assembly

Line 6 ramekins, straight-sided old-fashioned glasses, a large pyramid mold, or a smooth-sided mold of your choice with bread cut to fit to the rim of the mold, leaving no open spaces. Spoon fruit and syrup into each mold, filling to the top. Top with a layer of bread cut to fit. Spoon sauce on top. Set the mold in a larger pan. Cover each with plastic wrap and weight it down with a 1- to 2-pound weight. (I have used the little disks that go on my workout bar, stones, bricks, small, heavy cans, whatever I had around the house.) Reserve any leftover juice. Chill for 24 hours.

To serve, unmold stacks onto serving plates, pour reserved juice over the stacks, and serve with additional fresh berries and crème fraîche.

Note: This is also wonderful as an Apple Charlotte Stack, using the buttered apples from Crepe Stacks with Buttered Apples, Almonds, and Stilton. Follow the same directions, using apples in the bread-lined mold instead of berries. Remember to saturate the bread with apple juices before weighting it down.

Poached Plums with Pound Cake, Lemon Curd, and Cinnamon Streusel

YIELD: 6 SERVINGS

This is one of my favorites. The rich plums, the lemon curd, and the pound cake create a terrific dessert. If plums are not in season, use dried plums that have been soaked to reconstitute. Also, try using other fruits: peaches, apricots, cherries, blueberries, bananas, kiwis, strawberries, or rapsberries.

Planning Ahead

- Make the plums and syrup the day before. Chill.
- Make the lemon curd 2 to 3 days before. Chill.
- Make the streusel 1 to 2 days before and store in a resealable plastic bag.

TIP: To thaw frozen or very cold butter, try grating it on a cheese grater. This makes it easier to cut the butter into a recipe.

PLUMS

1 cup Pinot Noir

1 cup port

$1/_2$ teaspoon cardamom

$1/_2$ teaspoon cinnamon

3 tablespoons brown sugar

1 tablespoon grated lemon zest

12 ripe red plums, halved, pitted, and sliced

CINNAMON STREUSEL

$1^1/_3$ cups all-purpose flour

$2/_3$ cup toasted pine nuts or almonds, sliced (page 161)

$1/_2$ cup brown sugar

1 teaspoon cinnamon

$1/_4$ teaspoon freshly grated nutmeg

Scant 1 cup butter

LEMON CURD

$1/_2$ cup butter

$1^1/_2$ cups superfine sugar

$1/_2$ cup freshly squeezed lemon juice

4 teaspoons grated lemon zest

5 eggs

1 pound cake (page 166)

18 plum slices, for garnish

$2/_3$ cup sweetened whipped cream, for garnish

6 mint sprigs, for garnish

Confectioners' sugar, for dusting

Advance Preparation

To make the plums, preheat the oven to 350°. Combine all of the plum ingredients and pour into a medium baking dish. Bake, uncovered, for 30 minutes. With a slotted spoon, transfer the plums to a separate dish. Pour the syrup into a saucepan and reduce over high heat for about 10 minutes, or until the syrup is thickened. Set aside. Slice the drained plums.

To make the streusel topping, combine the flour, pine nuts, brown sugar, cinnamon, and nutmeg and mix well. Cut or grate in the butter and rub together with the other ingredients until it resembles chunky oatmeal. Grease a shallow dish and pat streusel in an even layer about $1/_2$ inch thick. Bake at 350° for 20 to 30 minutes, or until the streusel is crispy and browned. Cool slightly, then break apart into small pieces.

To make the lemon curd, melt the butter in a saucepan and add the sugar over medium-high heat. Stir until the sugar is dissolved. Add the lemon juice and zest and cook 1 minute. Remove from the heat. Whip the eggs and stir $1/_2$ cup of the hot liquid into the eggs to warm them up (this prevents curdling). Slowly whisk the warmed eggs into the hot lemon sauce. Return to the heat, stirring constantly, until the mixture thickens, 10 to 15 minutes. Keep the heat low—do not boil or the eggs will curdle. Remove from the heat. Cool and chill.

Assembly

Cut the pound cake into $1/_2$-inch slices. Then cut each slice into a 3-inch round. You will need 18 rounds. (You may have to patch slices together to form a whole round.) Frost each slice with 1 tablespoon of lemon curd. Layer in the following order: 1 slice frosted pound cake, 3 to 4 slices plums, 2 tablespoons streusel, 1 tablespoon plum syrup. Repeat and top with a third cake slice. Press down firmly but gently. Frost with lemon curd. Chill stacks.

To serve, slide a spatula under each stack and transfer to a serving plate. Unmold, garnish with additional lemon curd, plums, whipped cream, and a sprig of mint. Dust with confectioners' sugar.

Note: Leftover streusel keeps very well in plastic bags in the freezer.

Shortcut Stacks

- Buy a quality lemon curd.
- Use a ready-made pound cake or a bakery pound cake.

S'Mores Stacks for Rosie O'Donnell

These stacks are a blast of nostalgia. Remember when you camped out in the backyard and made s'mores over a fire? If not, now you can taste the same thing in a most sophisticated way. If you want to make mini s'mores like in the photo, use $1^1/_2$ by 3-inch cylinders.

Planning Ahead

Good news! These have to be made ahead!

- Make the graham cracker cake up to 1 week ahead. Wrap well in plastic wrap and freeze. Thaw before cutting the rounds.
- Make the chocolate filling up to 2 days in advance. Chill. Warm before assembling the stacks.
- Assemble the stacks several days ahead and freeze.

GRAHAM CRACKER CRUMB CAKE

1 cup butter, room temperature

$1^2/_3$ cups sugar

4 eggs, separated

$3^1/_4$ cups graham cracker crumbs

1 teaspoon baking powder

$1^1/_2$ cups whole milk

1 teaspoon vanilla

CHOCOLATE FILLING

2 tablespoons sweet butter

$1/_4$ cup packed dark brown sugar

2 tablespoons light corn syrup

$1/_2$ cup peanut butter

$2/_3$ cup chopped semisweet chocolate

$1/_2$ cup heavy whipping cream

1 teaspoon vanilla

$1^1/_2$ cups miniature marshmallows

1 quart pralines-and-cream ice cream

$1/_2$ cup ground English toffee

Confectioners' sugar, for dusting

Advance Preparation

To make the cake, preheat the oven to 350°.

Butter a 12 by 17-inch sheet pan and line with parchment. Cream together the butter and sugar until fluffy. Add the egg yolks 1 at a time, beating after each addition. Mix the graham crackers and baking powder together and add to the butter mixture. Mix well. Add the milk and vanilla and blend well. Beat the egg whites until stiff and fold gently into the batter. Pour the batter into the prepared pan and smooth. Bake at 350° for 25 minutes, or until the cake begins to pull away from the edge of the pan. Cool and invert onto a rack to cool completely. Cut 18 3-inch rounds from the cake. Set aside.

To make the chocolate filling, melt the butter, sugar, and corn syrup in a medium saucepan. Stir until blended and bring to a boil. Decrease the heat to medium. Add the peanut butter and chocolate and stir until melted and blended. Whisk in the cream and vanilla and simmer for 2 minutes. The sauce can be used at once or poured into a glass jar and stored in the refrigerator for up to 1 month.

To toast the marshmallows, spread the marshmallows very close together on a foil-lined sheet pan. Place under the broiler and toast until golden brown. Or use a small propane blowtorch (available at hardware stores or gourmet supply stores). Aim the torch, set on low, at the marshmallows, using a back and forth sweeping motion, until the marshmallows are toasted. (If you use the blowtorch, read the instructions carefully and keep out of reach of children. Blowtorches are also handy for meringues, crème brûlée, and crumb toppings.)

Note: See Resources, page 169, for blowtorches. Surfas Gourmet Foods and Professional Cookware in Los Angeles has a new, small blowtorch for home use. You can mail-order it.

Assembly

Spray 6 stack cylinders with vegetable spray and place on a sheet pan. Spread approximately 1 tablespoon of chocolate sauce on each of the 12 cake rounds. Working quickly, layer in the following order: 1 cake and chocolate round, 2 teaspoons crushed English Toffee, 1 tablespoon toasted mini marshmallows, 1 small scoop slightly softened ice cream. Repeat the layers and top with a plain cake round. Press down gently but firmly. Freeze immediately.

To serve, remove the stacks from the freezer and let stand for 5 minutes. Slide a spatula under each stack and transfer to a serving plate. Unmold. Working quickly, top each stack with a solid layer of toasted marshmallows. Surround with a drizzle of extra chocolate sauce, sift confectioners' sugar over all, and serve immediately.

Shortcut Stacks

Buy a 16-ounce jar of quality chocolate sauce, warm it, and mix in $1/_2$ cup peanut butter. Blend well and chill.

Mango, Pound Cake, and Mascarpone Stacks

YIELD: 6 SERVINGS

This is one of the easiest recipes in this book. If you use the shortcut, it literally takes minutes to prepare and never fails to dazzle guests. Make this when mangoes are at their peak, during the summer.

Planning Ahead

Assemble the stacks early in the day and chill.

1 large pound cake, sliced into 12 $1/_2$-inch slices (page 166)

8 ounces mascarpone cheese

1 cup crushed chocolate-covered English toffee

3 mangoes, peeled, seeded, and coarsely chopped

$1^1/_4$ cups caramel sauce (page 168)

Confectioners' sugar, for dusting

Assembly

Spray 6 stack cylinders with vegetable spray and place them on a sheet pan. With a 3-inch cutter or stack cylinder, cut the pound cake slices into rounds. (You may have to piece the rounds together.) Spread each round generously with about $1^1/_2$ tablespoons mascarpone. Layer in the following order: 1 frosted pound cake round, 2 tablespoons toffee, 2 tablespoons mango, 1 tablespoon caramel sauce, drizzled over the mangoes. Repeat. Press down firmly but gently and chill for at least 1 hour.

To serve, slide a spatula under each stack cylinder and transfer to a serving plate. Unmold, drizzle with additional caramel, and top with any leftover mangoes and toffee. Dust the whole presentation with confectioners' sugar and serve.

Shortcut Stacks

• Purchase a quality caramel sauce.

• A ready-made pound cake works well for this recipe.

Fourth of July Sweet Stacks with Raspberry Coulis

YIELD: 6 SERVINGS

The first time I served this stack was during an outdoor summer concert, at intermission. This will cause a sensation, particularly with sparklers on top as garnish. Use any choice of fresh berries.

Planning Ahead

- Make the raspberry coulis the day before and chill.
- Assemble the stacks in the afternoon and chill.

TIP: If you cannot find berry honey, substitute $1/2$ cup honey and $1/2$ cup blueberry preserves warmed and mixed together. Berry honey is available in many gourmet markets, or order from Bristol Farms. See Resources, page 170.

RASPBERRY COULIS

2 pints fresh raspberries, washed, dried, and picked over

4 tablespoons sugar

3 tablespoons water

ANGEL FOOD CAKE

1 cup sifted cake flour

$1^1/_2$ cups superfine sugar

12 egg whites

$1^1/_2$ teaspoons cream of tartar

$1/_4$ teaspoon salt

$1^1/_2$ teaspoons vanilla

$3/_4$ cup mascarpone cheese

1 pint fresh raspberries, washed, dried, and picked over

$1/_2$ cup berry honey, warmed

6 pieces chocolate-covered English toffee, ground in a food processor

1 pint fresh blueberries, washed, dried, and picked over

Confectioners' sugar, for dusting

White chocolate curls, for garnish (optional)

Fourth of July sparkler, for garnish (optional)

Advance Preparation

To make the coulis, boil the raspberries, sugar, and water together for 1 minute. Decrease the heat and simmer 20 minutes, crushing berries with a wooden spoon. Strain, pressing juice out of the solids. Return to the stove and simmer 20 additional minutes. Cover and chill.

To make the angel food cake, preheat the oven to 375°. Sift the flour with $3/4$ cup superfine sugar 4 times. With an electric mixer, beat the egg whites with the cream of tartar and salt until frothy. Add the vanilla and beat until soft peaks form. Add the remaining $3/4$ cup sugar, 1 tablespoon at a time, and continue beating until the meringue is stiff and glossy. Sift one quarter of the flour mixture over the egg whites and fold in. Fold in the remaining flour $1/4$ cup at a time, using a gentle under/over folding motion. Pour into an ungreased 10-inch tube pan. Bake at 375° for 35 to 40 minutes. Remove from the oven, invert the pan, and allow the cake to cool.

Assembly

Cut the angel food cake into horizontal $1/2$-inch slices. Using a 3-inch-round stack cylinder or a 3-inch cutter, cut out 18 rounds from cake layers. (Freeze leftover cake for another use.) Frost each round with 1 tablespoon of mascarpone. Spray 6 stack cylinders with vegetable spray and place them on a sheet pan. Layer in the following order: 1 frosted angel food round, a layer of raspberries, 2 teaspoons honey, 1 tablespoon toffee. Repeat, using blueberries for the second layer, and top with an angel food round. Press down firmly but gently, then frost the top cake round with mascarpone. Mix together the remaining berries. Top each stack with 3 tablespoons of berries and 2 teaspoons of honey. Chill 1 hour or longer.

To serve, spoon $1/4$ cup raspberry coulis onto each of 6 plates. Transfer the stacks to each plate. Unmold and garnish with any remaining berries, a dusting of confectioners' sugar, chocolate curls, and a lit sparkler. Serve immediately.

TIP: To achieve a beautiful dusting of confectioners' sugar, place the sugar in a small strainer and sprinkle over stacks.

Tapioca, Plum, and Caramel Stacks

YIELD: 6 SERVINGS

I made this stack with plums, but almost any fruit would be delicious, making this a year-round recipe. Try grilled apple slices, peaches, bananas, pineapple, or pears.

Planning Ahead

- Make the tapioca 1 day ahead and chill.
- Make the puff pastries early in the day.
- Grill the plums 2 hours before assembling stacks.

TAPIOCA

$2^1/_2$ tablespoons superfine sugar

$2^1/_2$ tablespoons brown sugar

2 cups milk

3 tablespoons quick-cooking tapioca

Pinch of salt

1 egg yolk

$1^1/_2$ teaspoons vanilla

1 egg white

$^1/_3$ cup mascarpone cheese or cream cheese

PUFF PASTRY

1 package frozen puff pastry sheets, defrosted in refrigerator

1 egg, lightly beaten

2 tablespoons milk

PLUMS

6 plums

$^1/_4$ cup honey

$^1/_4$ teaspoon cardamom

$^1/_4$ teaspoon cinnamon

1 cup caramel sauce (page 168)

Confectioners' sugar, for dusting

Advance Preparation

To make the tapioca, reserve 2 tablespoons of superfine sugar and combine the remaining sugar and brown sugar with $1^1/_2$ cups milk, tapioca, and salt. Let stand 10 minutes. Bring to a boil over medium-high heat, stirring constantly. Remove from the heat. Whisk the remaining $^1/_2$ cup milk with the egg yolk and 1 teaspoon vanilla and slowly add to the pudding. Beat the egg white to soft peaks, add the reserved 2 tablespoons sugar, and beat to stiff peaks. Fold into the slightly cooled pudding. Let rest 15 minutes, then whip in the mascarpone and the remaining $^1/_2$ teaspoon vanilla. Chill for 2 to 3 hours, or until thick and cold. (It should be thick but not pasty.)

Preheat the oven to 375°.

To make the puff pastry, place a pastry sheet on a floured surface and cut into 18 6-inch circles, or a shape of your choice. Try square, triangle, or diamond shapes. Prick all over with a fork. Mix the egg and milk and brush it on the sheet, being careful not to allow the egg wash to run down the sides of the raw pastry. (This would keep the pastry from rising evenly as it cooks.) Bake for 15 minutes, or until golden. Set aside.

To make the plums, cut the plums in half lengthwise. Brush with honey and sprinkle lightly with cardamom and cinnamon. Grill or broil the plums until golden, about 10 minutes. Cut each half into thirds. You'll have 36 plum pieces.

Assembly

Place 1 puff pastry circle on each of 6 plates. Spoon 2 tablespoons tapioca over the pastry. Top with 3 pieces of the plums, then drizzle with caramel sauce. Repeat the layers and top with a third pastry disk.

To serve, drizzle with caramel. Sprinkle with confectioners' sugar and serve immediately.

Shortcut Stacks

- Purchase the tapioca from a gourmet market or deli.
- Purchase a quality caramel sauce.

TIP: To achieve professional-looking drizzles and squiggles, place your sauce (sweet or savory) in a plastic squeeze bottle fitted with a narrow tip. With this method you can create dots, lines, circles, and drizzles without any mess.

Raspberry-Lemon Meringue Stacks

YIELD: 6 SERVINGS

This is a perfect dessert for a bridal shower or a formal luncheon. The combination of raspberries and lemon is sublime; also try blueberries, kiwis, apricots, strawberries—the sky's the limit.

Planning Ahead

• Make the meringues the day before or early in the day.

• Prepare the lemon curd the day before.

TIP: To load a pastry bag without mess, try using an ice cream scoop.

MERINGUE

5 tablespoons plus $1/3$ cup superfine sugar

$2/3$ cup confectioners' sugar

5 egg whites, room temperature

LEMON CURD FILLING

$1/2$ cup butter

$1^1/_2$ cups superfine sugar

$1/2$ cup freshly squeezed lemon juice

4 teaspoons lemon zest

5 eggs

2 pints fresh raspberries

1 tablespoon lemon zest, for garnish

$2/3$ cup additional fresh raspberries, for garnish

Advance Preparation

To make the meringues, line 2 large sheet pans with parchment paper and lightly outline 18 3-inch star shapes on the paper. (A star cookie cutter works well.) Spray the parchment with vegetable spray.

Sift $1^1/_2$ tablespoons superfine sugar with $2/3$ cup confectioners' sugar. Set aside.

Place the egg whites in a large, preferably copper, bowl. Beat the egg whites until frothy. Add $3^1/_2$ tablespoons superfine sugar and continue beating until soft peaks form. Slowly add $1/3$ cup superfine sugar and continue to beat until meringue holds stiff peaks. Gently fold in the sifted confectioners' sugar using a wide spatula. Fit a pastry bag with a $1/_2$-inch plain tip and fill the bag with meringue. Pipe the meringue onto the prepared star outlines, forming solid star shapes. For a garnish, pipe 6 large and 6 small additional star shapes with the meringue, leaving the center space open. Bake at 200° for 75 to 90 minutes, or until firm to the touch. You will need 18 stars. Let cool.

To make the lemon curd, melt the butter in a medium saucepan and add the sugar. Over medium-high heat, stir the butter and sugar until dissolved. Add the lemon juice and zest and cook 1 minute. Remove from the heat. Whip the eggs. Pour about $1/2$ cup of the hot liquid into the eggs to warm them up (this prevents curdling). Slowly whisk the warmed eggs into the hot lemon sauce. Return to the heat, stirring constantly until the mixture thickens, 10 to 15 minutes. Keep the heat low. Do not boil or the eggs may curdle. Cool and refrigerate until needed.

Assembly

Place a solid meringue star on each of 6 serving plates. Top with 3 tablespoons lemon curd. Top curd with a single layer of raspberries. Repeat, using 3 stars per serving and ending with a dollop of lemon curd.

To serve, garnish with lemon zest and fresh raspberries. Top with the open star meringue and serve immediately.

Shortcut Stacks

- Purchase the meringue stars or disks from your local bakery. Call to special order.

- Purchase a quality lemon curd.

Summer Trifle Stacks

YIELD: 6 SERVINGS

I love the look of this stack. The colors are wonderful. One of the advantages of this stack is you can substitute different fruits. You can even use just one type of fruit. Think all raspberry or kiwi or strawberry— you decide!

Planning Ahead

- Make the custard and mix with the mascarpone 1 day ahead. Chill.

- Slice the fruit. Chill.

- Crush the amaretti biscuits up to 2 days ahead.

- Make stacks 2 to 4 hours ahead and chill.

1 large pound cake, cut into $^1/_2$-inch slices (page 166)

$^3/_4$ cup raspberry or apricot liqueur

1 cup quality apricot preserves

$1^1/_2$ cups thick vanilla custard (or powdered instant vanilla custard), chilled

1 cup pitted and chopped fresh apricots, nectarines, or peaches

1 cup crushed amaretti biscuits

1 cup fresh raspberries or blueberries

$^1/_2$ cup mascarpone cheese

6 kiwis, peeled and sliced, for garnish

1 cup whipped cream, for garnish

Advance Preparation

With a stack cylinder or 3-inch cutter, cut the pound cake slices into rounds. You will need a total of 12 rounds and may need to piece the rounds together. Lightly sprinkle one side of each round with the liqueur, then spread with the preserves. Set aside.

Mix together the chilled custard and mascarpone until smooth. Set aside.

TIP: An easy way to sprinkle liqueur over a cake is to pour liquid into a small, clean spray bottle, then simply spritz the liqueur over the cake rounds.

Assembly

Spray 6 stack cylinders with vegetable spray and place them on a sheet pan. Layer in the following order: 1 pound cake round, 2 tablespoons apricots, 2 tablespoons custard, 1 tablespoon crushed amaretti, 1 pound cake round (press down gently but firmly), 2 tablespoons berries, 2 tablespoons custard, 1 tablespoon crushed amaretti. Press down again. Refrigerate for 2 to 4 hours to allow flavors to blend.

To serve, slide a spatula under each stack cylinder and transfer to a serving plate. Unmold, garnish with sliced kiwis, whipped cream, and any additional leftover berries and amaretti, and serve.

Winter Dried Fruit Compote Stacks

YIELD: 6 SERVINGS

I adore dried fruit compote with cinnamon and brown sugar. One day, I made a compote and served it with roast pork. A new dessert stack was born.

Planning Ahead

- Make the compote up to 2 days ahead and chill.

- Make the crème fraîche 1 day ahead and chill.

- Assemble up to 4 hours ahead and chill (can be warmed in a 350° oven for 5 minutes before serving).

FRUIT

2$^1/_2$ cups chopped dried mixed fruit (apricots, apples, pears, prunes, peaches)

$^1/_2$ cup dried cranberries

$^1/_2$ cup brown sugar

1 stick cinnamon

$^1/_4$ teaspoon freshly ground nutmeg

Zest of $^1/_2$ orange

2 to 3 cups water

ORANGE CRÈME FRAÎCHE

1 cup crème fraîche

Zest of $^1/_2$ orange

Juice from $^1/_2$ orange

1 large pound cake, cut into $^1/_2$-inch slices (page 166)

$^3/_4$ cup mascarpone cheese

$^3/_4$ cup toasted almonds (page 161)

$^1/_2$ cup additional almonds, for garnish

Advance Preparation

To make the fruit, mix the fruit and all ingredients together. Place in a large saucepan, bring to a boil, decrease the heat, and simmer for 1 hour, or until slightly thickened. Cool. Remove the cinnamon stick. Drain, reserving syrup. If the fruit is dry, add more liquid to give it the consistency of thick soup. You will need the reserved syrup for the recipe.

To make the crème fraîche, mix together the ingredients and chill.

Assembly

Spray 6 stack cylinders with vegetable spray and place them on a sheet pan. With a 3-inch cutter, cut 12 rounds from the cake slices. (You may have to piece the rounds together.) Frost each round with 1 tablespoon mascarpone. Layer in the following order: 1 frosted pound cake round, 2 tablespoons drained fruit, 1 tablespoon toasted almonds, 1 frosted pound cake round (press down gently but firmly), 2 tablespoons drained fruit, 1 tablespoon toasted almonds. Chill for at least 1 hour.

To serve, slide a spatula under each stack cylinder and transfer to a serving plate. Unmold, garnish with crème fraîche, 2 tablespoons reserved fruit syrup, and additional almonds, and serve.

Chocolate Bread Pudding Stacks with Fresh Cherry Sauce

YIELD: 6 SERVINGS

In the first chapter of this book I described being at the Irvine Amphitheater last summer, serving Chocolate Bread Pudding Stacks, when a woman came climbing over the chairs to ask me what I was serving. At that moment I realized this recipe was a must for this book! This makes a great dessert for a picnic, served at room temperature. It's also great with a side of ice cream, sweetened whipped cream or berry sorbet.

Planning Ahead

- Prepare the bread pudding the day before.
- Prepare the cherry sauce the day before. Chill.
- Toast the hazelnuts 2 to 3 days before. Freeze.
- Stacks can be assembled early in the day and chilled.

TIP: The secret to good bread pudding is the bread. Do not use "airy" bread—thick, heavy bread or pannetone works best.

BREAD PUDDING

1¹/₂ cups half-and-half

1 cup heavy whipping cream

1 cup shaved or chopped semisweet chocolate

1 cup sugar

2 large eggs

1¹/₂ teaspoons vanilla

8 cups 1-inch bread cubes (use day-old panettone, French, or a very firm white country bread), crusts removed

CHERRY SAUCE

1 pound fresh cherries, pitted, or 2 cups dried cherries, soaked in hot water to reconstitute

Pinch of cinnamon

3 tablespoons Chambord raspberry liqueur (or a raspberry syrup)

¹/₄ cup sugar

¹/₂ teaspoon vanilla

³/₄ cup toasted hazelnuts (page 161)

Shaved chocolate, for garnish

Additional cherries, for garnish

Confectioners' sugar, for dusting

Advance Preparation

To make the bread pudding, preheat the oven to 350°.

Combine the half-and-half and cream in a medium saucepan and bring to a simmer. Remove from the heat. Place the chocolate in a large bowl and pour the hot cream over it, stirring until the chocolate is smooth and blended. Beat the eggs and sugar together, add the vanilla, and slowly stir into the chocolate. Blend well. Toss the bread cubes in the chocolate until well coated. Pour into a greased 9 by 13-inch pan and let sit for 10 to 15 minutes. Bake for 30 minutes, or until the pudding is set and slightly puffed. Remove from the oven and cool. Cut into 9 3-inch rounds. Cut the rounds in half horizontally. Set aside.

To make the cherry sauce, place all of the ingredients in a saucepan and bring to a boil, decrease to a simmer, and cook gently for 15 to 20 minutes. Cool sauce and refrigerate until needed.

Assembly

Spray 6 stack cylinders with vegetable spray and place them on a sheet pan. Layer in the following order: 1 chocolate bread pudding round, 2 tablespoons slightly drained cherries, 1 tablespoon toasted hazelnuts, 1 chocolate bread pudding round (press down gently but firmly), 2 tablespoons slightly drained cherries, 1 tablespoon toasted hazelnuts. Top with the third bread pudding round. Press down gently. Chill until serving.

To serve cold, slide a spatula under each stack cylinder and transfer to a serving plate. Unmold and garnish with shaved chocolate, additional cherry sauce and cherries, and a dusting of confectioners' sugar.

To serve warm, bake at 350° for 10 to 15 minutes, place on plates, unmold, and garnish.

Shortcut Stacks

Order chocolate bread pudding from your bakery.

Almond Meringues with Mangoes, Strawberries, and Kiwis

YIELD: 6 SERVINGS

Meringues and fruit are not only low in fat, but also visually impressive.

Planning Ahead

- Make meringues the day before or early in the day.

- Slice and chill the fruit. Whip the cream with a stabilizer called "Whip It" (available in fine markets), and chill.

- For a low-fat version, use only fruit and meringues, with just a dollop of cream on top.

MERINGUES

$1/_2$ cup plus $1/_3$ cup superfine sugar

$2/_3$ cup confectioners' sugar

5 egg whites, room temperature

$1/_4$ cup ground toasted almonds (page 161)

$3^3/_4$ cups whipped cream

2 cups sliced mangoes

2 cups sliced strawberries

$3/_4$ cup sliced kiwis (about 2 kiwis), for garnish

Advance Preparation

To make the meringues, line 2 large sheet pans with parchment paper and lightly draw 18 3-inch circles on the paper. Spray the circles with vegetable spray.

Sift $1^1/_2$ tablespoons superfine sugar with $2/_3$ cup confectioners' sugar. Set aside.

Place the egg whites in a large, preferably copper, bowl. Beat the egg whites until frothy. Add $2^1/_2$ tablespoons superfine sugar and continue beating until soft peaks form. Slowly add $1/_3$ cup superfine sugar and continue to beat until the meringue holds stiff peaks. Gently fold in the sifted confectioners' sugar using a wide spatula. Gently fold in the almonds. Fit a pastry bag with a plain $1/_2$-inch tip and fill the bag with meringue. Beginning at the center of each 3-inch circle, pipe the meringue, forming a round disk. Bake at 200° for 75 to 90 minutes, or until firm to the touch. Do not let meringues brown; if they look like they are browning, turn the oven down to 175°. Let cool.

Mix the whipped cream with the remaining superfine sugar. Set aside.

Assembly

Place a meringue disk on each of 6 plates. Top with $1/_4$ cup sweetened whipped cream and smooth. Top the cream with mangoes, then place another disk on top. Spread another $1/_4$ cup whipped cream and top with strawberries. Place a third disk on top of the strawberries and top with 2 tablespoons of whipped cream. Garnish decoratively with kiwis. Serve immediately.

Crepe Stacks with Buttered Apples, Almonds, and Stilton

YIELD: 6 SERVINGS

The idea of layers and layers of crepes appealed to me for stacks, and the flavor combination of apples, Stilton, and crepes is just sensational. This is also a stack that can be made in a 9-inch springform pan as a stack crepe cake for special occasions. Simply prepare 9-inch crepes instead of 3-inch. This dessert is also ideal for picnics—it travels well and tastes perfect at room temperature.

Planning Ahead

- Prepare the crepes as much as 1 week ahead and freeze between layers of waxed paper. Thaw before using.

- Prepare the apples and toasted almonds the day before.

- Prepare the crème fraîche the day before.

- Assemble the stacks the day before and chill.

- Prepare the caramel sauce up to 5 days ahead and chill. Warm before using.

CREPES

4 eggs

1 cup sifted all-purpose flour

2 tablespoons sugar

$1^1/_2$ cups milk (or more to thin down batter)

$^1/_4$ cup water

1 tablespoon melted butter

2 teaspoons vanilla

$^1/_2$ cup clarified butter (page 161)

APPLES

4 tablespoons butter

$^1/_4$ cup light rum

$^1/_3$ cup evaporated milk

$^1/_2$ cup brown sugar

$^1/_2$ cup honey

12 tart green apples, peeled, cored, and sliced

$^3/_4$ cup apricot preserves

$^1/_2$ cup toasted almonds, sliced (page 161)

$^1/_2$ cup crumbled Stilton cheese

$^3/_4$ cup Lemon Crème Fraîche (recipe follows)

1 cup caramel sauce (page 168)

1 apple, cut into paper-thin slices, for garnish

Advance Preparation

To make the crepes, combine eggs, flour, sugar, milk, water, melted butter, and vanilla in a food processor and blend well. Refrigerate for 1 to 2 hours. Heat a small skillet or crepe pan and brush very lightly with melted clarified butter. Pour 2 tablespoons batter into the hot skillet and cook until the edges are dry and the top bubbles begin to break. Flip over and cook for 30 seconds longer. Place crepe on a plate. Repeat, using all the batter. Any leftover crepes freeze beautifully. Trim crepes to 3-inch rounds. You will need 36 crepes for this recipe.

Crepe Stacks with Buttered Apples, Almonds, and Stilton cont.

To make the apples, melt the butter in a large pot. Add the rum, milk, sugar, and honey. Bring to a boil. Add the apples, bring to a gentle boil, and cook for a few minutes, then pour into a large, shallow baking dish. Cover. Bake covered at 350° for 20 minutes. Uncover, raise the temperature to 375°, and bake 30 additional minutes, basting every 10 minutes. Remove from the oven and cool. Reserve the sauce for garnish.

In a small saucepan, warm the apricot preserves until melted. Pour warm preserves through a medium strainer to remove the whole pieces of apricot. Set the strained preserves glaze aside.

Assembly

Spray 6 stack cylinders with vegetable spray and place them on a sheet pan. Spread each 3-inch crepe with apricot preserves glaze. Layer stacks in the following order: 1 crepe, 1½ tablespoons apples, 1 teaspoon almonds. Repeat for 2 more crepes. When layering the fourth crepe, add 1 tablespoon Stilton cheese with the other ingredients. You will add Stilton only once at this point. Continue layering: crepe, apples, almonds, until all remaining crepes are used, ending with the sixth crepe. Press down gently but firmly. Crepe stacks may now be chilled and can be made several hours in advance.

To serve cold, slide a spatula under each stack cylinder and transfer to a serving plate. Unmold, spoon any remaining apple-sauce from the apples around the crepe, and garnish with Lemon Crème Fraîche, drizzled carmel sauce, and thin apple slices, if desired.

To serve warm, bake at 350° for 10 to 15 minutes. Place on plates, unmold, and garnish.

Note: For fun, make a large crepe, fit it into a pyramid mold, fill with apples, and top with a second crepe cut to fit the mold. Suspend the mold in a bowl or pitcher, cover it with plastic wrap, weight it down, and chill for 24 hours. To serve, unmold onto a serving plate and garnish with apple slices, caramel sauce, and confectioners' sugar.

Shortcut Stacks

- Use frozen scalloped apples, sliced or chopped.
- Buy a quality caramel sauce.
- Purchase crepes from your favorite bakery.

LEMON CRÈME FRAÎCHE
YIELD: 1 CUP

1 cup crème fraîche

Zest of ½ lemon

2 tablespoons freshly squeezed lemon juice

3 tablespoons sugar

Mix ingredients together and chill.

Death by Chocolate

Well! You just know I had to put something totally decadent as the final recipe. My advice? Diet on your own time!

Planning Ahead

- Prepare the brownies 1 day ahead.
- Assemble the stacks early in the day and chill.

FILLING

$1/2$ cup semisweet chocolate, cut into chunks and melted in the top of a double boiler

1 cup whipped cream

$1/2$ cup crushed chocolate-covered English toffee

$1/2$ cup mascarpone cheese

9 Fab's Brownies, cut into 3-inch rounds (page 167)

3 pints fresh raspberries, washed and dried

$3/4$ cup chocolate sauce (page 167), for garnish

Confectioners' sugar, for dusting

Advance Preparation

Mix together the cooled (not cold) chocolate, the whipped cream, toffee, and mascarpone, stirring to blend. Chill for 30 minutes.

Assembly

Spray 6 stack cylinders with vegetable spray and place them on a sheet pan. Cut each brownie in half for a total of 18 rounds. Layer in the following order: 1 brownie round, 1 tablespoon chocolate filling, 1 layer raspberries. Repeat and top with a third brownie round. Press down gently but firmly. Spread 1 more tablespoon of the chocolate filling on top and arrange another layer of berries. Chill until serving.

To serve, remove stacks from the refrigerator one half hour before serving. Slide a spatula under each stack cylinder and transfer to a serving plate. Unmold, garnish with chocolate sauce, a generous dusting of confectioners' sugar, and additional berries if desired.

Shortcut Stacks

Purchase the brownies from a good bakery.

STACK BASICS

Lemon Vinaigrette

YIELD: ABOUT 1 CUP

This is a good dressing for a salad, but it is also a good marinade for fish or chicken, minus the cream.

1/4 cup freshly squeezed lemon juice

2 tablespoons minced chives

2 teaspoons lemon zest

1 tablespoon herb mustard

3/4 cup extra virgin olive oil

1 tablespoon heavy whipping cream

1 tablespoon minced fresh parsley

Whisk together the lemon juice, chives, zest, and mustard until smooth. Slowly add the oil while whisking until the dressing thickens. Add the cream and blend. Stir in the parsley. This dressing will keep 3 to 4 days, covered and refrigerated.

Balsamic Vinaigrette

YIELD: 1 CUP

1 tablespoon Dijon mustard

1 clove garlic, minced

1/4 teaspoon salt

1/8 teaspoon freshly ground black pepper

1/4 cup balsamic vinegar

3/4 cup extra virgin olive oil

In a small bowl, whisk together the mustard, garlic, salt, and pepper. Add the vinegar and whisk well. Slowly pour in the oil while whisking to blend and thicken. This dressing will keep 1 to 2 weeks in the refrigerator.

Oven-Roasted Tomatoes

YIELD: ABOUT 2 CUPS

These tomatoes are a perfect complement to many stacks combinations. They can be used in a sauce or as a layer with beef, chicken, pasta, polenta, potatoes, or grilled vegetables. They are also quite good with salad greens, some Gorgonzola, and a tomato vinaigrette.

12 Roma tomatoes, halved lengthwise

1/2 cup extra virgin olive oil

2 tablespoons sugar

1 tablespoon minced fresh rosemary

Salt and freshly ground black pepper to taste

Preheat the oven to 200°.

Place the tomatoes, cut side up, on 2 lightly greased sheet pans. Drizzle the tomatoes with olive oil. Season with sugar, rosemary, salt, and pepper.

Place the sheet pan in the oven and roast for 4 to 6 hours, or until the tomatoes are just beginning to dry out but are still pulpy and rich looking. Cool. The tomatoes may be stored covered in the refrigerator for up to 1 week.

Mango Salsa

YIELD: ABOUT 2¹/₂ CUPS

Try this with grilled shrimp, fish, or chicken for a simple and fresh dinner combination.

1¹/₂ mangoes, peeled and diced

¹/₄ pineapple, peeled and diced

3 tablespoons diced red onion

1 orange, peeled and diced

¹/₄ red bell pepper, seeded and diced

3 tablespoons chopped fresh cilantro

1 tablespoon freshly squeezed lime juice

¹/₈ teaspoon red pepper flakes, or to taste

¹/₈ teaspoon ground white pepper

Combine all ingredients in a glass bowl. Stir well, cover, and chill for 1 to 2 hours. The salsa will keep for 2 days in the refrigerator.

Tomato Salsa

YIELD: ABOUT 3 CUPS

2 cloves garlic, minced

1 onion, chopped

1 (7-ounce) can chiles, chopped

8 tomatoes, seeded and chopped

¹/₂ red bell pepper, seeded and chopped

4 scallions, chopped

3 tablespoons vegetable oil

1¹/₂ tablespoons vinegar

2 teaspoons sugar

¹/₂ cup chopped cilantro

3 tablespoons chopped fresh parsley

Salt and freshly ground black pepper to taste

Mix together the garlic, onion, chiles, tomatoes, bell pepper, and scallions in a large glass or noncorrosive bowl. Whisk together the oil, vinegar, and sugar and pour over vegetables. Stir in the cilantro and parsley. Season with salt and pepper to taste. Cover and refrigerate. The salsa will keep for 2 days in the refrigerator.

TIP: Salsas work very well with stacks. Try using your imagination and creativity when matching salsas to various flavors. For example, try

- Jalapeño, black bean, and corn salsa with grilled tuna, chicken, or swordfish
- Pineapple-cucumber salsa with grilled chicken or pork
- Peach salsa with pork, ribs, turkey, or duck
- Mango salsa with salmon, shrimp, or chicken
- Tomato and roasted pepper salsa with swordfish or grilled steak

Italian Tomato Sauce

YIELD: 5 TO 6 CUPS

This sauce can be used for a wide variety of stacks. It is also great over pasta—and freezes beautifully.

2 tablespoons extra virgin olive oil

1 cup chopped onion

1 leek, white part only, chopped

3 cloves garlic, minced

$1/2$ cup chopped celery

$1/2$ cup dry red wine

3 cups peeled, seeded, and chopped tomatoes

4 tablespoons tomato paste

2 cups beef stock

3 tablespoons chopped fresh oregano

3 tablespoons chopped fresh rosemary

1 bay leaf

$1/8$ teaspoon allspice

$2/3$ cup chopped Italian parsley

3 tablespoons chopped fresh basil

4 tablespoons light corn syrup

Heat the olive oil in a large pot. Sauté the onion and leek for 5 minutes. Add the garlic and celery and sauté 5 minutes longer. Add the wine, tomatoes, and tomato paste. Cook for a few minutes, blending well. Add the remaining ingredients, bring to a boil, decrease the heat to a simmer, and gently simmer, stirring occasionally, for 3 hours, or until the sauce is thick and rich. Ladle into small resealable plastic bags, label, and freeze for up to 6 months. The sauce can be stored in the refrigerator for 1 week.

Pesto

YIELD: 1 CUP

3 cups fresh basil, packed

4 cloves garlic

$3/4$ cup extra virgin olive oil

$1/2$ cup freshly grated Parmesan cheese

$1/2$ cup toasted pine nuts (page 161)

2 tablespoons heavy whipping cream

Place the basil and garlic in a food processor and chop very fine. Slowly add the olive oil. Using an on-off motion, pulse in the Parmesan and pine nuts. Add the cream and pulse to blend. Store the pesto covered in the refrigerator for up to 4 days.

Basil Oil

YIELD: 1 CUP

1 cup extra virgin olive oil

$2/3$ cup fresh basil

In a small saucepan, warm the olive oil over low heat; do not boil. Crush the basil in a glass bowl to release its flavor. Pour the warm oil over the basil and allow to stand at room temperature for 1 to 4 hours. Strain through two thicknesses of cheesecloth into a glass jar. The oil will keep in the refrigerator 3 to 4 weeks.

Note: You can use different herbs to make other types of infused oils.

Chicken Stock

YIELD: 4 QUARTS

2 whole small chickens, cut into pieces

3 onions, peeled and cut into quarters

6 carrots, scrubbed and cut into 3-inch
pieces

6 celery stalks, cut into 3-inch pieces

1 tablespoon salt

10 peppercorns

1 bay leaf

Place the chickens in a large stock pot and cover with water. Bring to a boil and skim off the foam. Add the remaining ingredients and simmer over low heat for 5 to 6 hours. Remove the chickens and vegetables and strain the stock through several thicknesses of cheesecloth. Chill. Remove cold stock from the refrigerator and remove the layer of congealed fat from the surface. Ladle stock into resealable plastic bags, label, and freeze.

Toasted Sesame Seeds

YIELD: 1 CUP

1 (9-ounce) jar sesame seeds

Place the sesame seeds in a small skillet over medium-high heat and cook, stirring, until seeds turn golden brown, about 5 minutes. Toasted seeds can be stored as you would the raw sesame seeds in a jar.

Toasted Walnuts, Pine Nuts, Almonds, or Pecans

YIELD: 2 CUPS

2 cups walnuts, pine nuts, almonds, or
pecans

Place the nuts in a small shallow baking pan and spread into an even layer. Bake in a 350° oven for about 8 minutes, or until the nuts are golden brown. Remove and cool. Can be frozen in resealable plastic bags.

Clarified Butter

YIELD: 1 CUP

1 pound butter

Melt the butter in a saucepan. Line a strainer with 3 thicknesses of cheesecloth and place over a bowl. Pour the hot butter through the cheesecloth, trapping the white "whey." You now have clear, clarified butter. Refrigerate, covered, for several weeks, using as needed. It will stay good for several months if frozen.

Wild Rice

YIELD: ABOUT 2 CUPS

1 cup wild rice

12 cups boiling water

2 tablespoons butter

Salt and freshly ground black pepper
    to taste

Rinse the rice several times with cold water. Place the rice in a large bowl and cover with 4 cups boiling water. Cover and let stand 20 minutes. Drain the rice and repeat to this point 2 more times, each time using 4 cups of fresh boiling water. Drain off any water. Fluff with a fork and season with the butter, salt, and pepper.

Sushi Rice

YIELD: ABOUT 4 1/2 CUPS

To make good sushi stacks, the sushi rice must be cooked properly. It is very easy to do; it just takes certain steps to ensure the right consistency.

3 1/2 cups Japanese (short-grain) rice

4 cups water

5 1/2 tablespoons Japanese rice vinegar

5 tablespoons sugar

1 tablespoon salt

Wash the rice several times and let it drain 1 hour in a colander. Place the drained rice in a large pot with a tight-fitting lid. Add the water, cover, and bring to a boil. Boil the rice, covered, for 1 1/2 minutes. Decrease the heat to medium and boil for 5 minutes. Decrease the heat to low and simmer about 15 minutes, or until the water is absorbed. Remove from the heat. Lift the lid and place a clean dish towel over the pot. Replace the lid and allow the rice to steam for 10 minutes.

Combine the rice vinegar, sugar, and salt in a saucepan and heat until the sugar dissolves (or use 6 tablespoons Japanese seasoned rice wine vinegar).

Spread the cooked rice over a nonmetallic tray or flat bowl and, with a flat paddle, begin to separate the rice grains. Slowly sprinkle the vinegar mixture over the grains as you continue to separate and stir the grains. As you continue, the rice must be cooled quickly. A hair dryer set on cool or a tabletop fan works very well. This cooling process, coupled with the vinegar, produces a beautiful sheen to the rice and keeps the grains separated. The rice will be somewhat sticky.

Keep rice at room temperature, covered with a clean towel until ready to use. Sushi rice works best when made the day of your party.

Note: You may also use a rice cooker to cook the rice. Then proceed with the cooling and separating instructions.

Mashed Potatoes

YIELD: 4 TO 5 CUPS

6 Yukon Gold potatoes, peeled and
quartered

3 tablespoons butter

$^1/_4$ cup milk

$^1/_4$ cup heavy whipping cream

Salt and freshly ground black pepper
to taste

Boil the potatoes for 20 minutes, or until tender. Drain and return to pan. Mash the potatoes roughly. Add the butter, milk, cream, salt, and pepper and whip the potatoes with a hand masher or hand mixer. Add more milk as needed. Mashed potatoes made for stacks should be fairly stiff and hold their shape.

Mashed Potato Variations

Try these combinations for a new treat.

BASIL POTATOES

Add 3 tablespoons freshly minced basil, along with 1 tablespoon freshly squeezed lemon juice.

SOUTHWESTERN POTATOES

Add 1 cup cooked, mashed carrots, $^1/_4$ cup chopped green onions, white part only, $^1/_4$ cup diced jalapeños, and 1 teaspoon cumin. Add $^1/_3$ cup sour cream in place of the cream. Blend well.

FENNEL POTATOES

Braise 2 cups sliced fennel in $^1/_2$ cup milk and $^1/_2$ cup cream until soft. Purée in a food processor. Then mash into the cooked potatoes, adding butter, salt, pepper, and 1 tablespoon lemon zest.

GARLIC POTATOES

Very gently sauté 2 to 3 cloves of garlic, very finely minced, in 2 tablespoons butter for 15 minutes. Add to the potatoes when mashing.

Polenta

YIELD: ONE 12 BY 17-INCH SHEET PAN
OR 6 SERVINGS

There are two types of polenta you can use for stacks. One is the original old-fashioned polenta that requires 40 minutes of cooking and stirring. The other is a newer, 5-minute version that seems to work quite nicely for stacks recipes.

1 (13^1/$_2$-ounce) package 5-minute polenta

2 tablespoons extra virgin olive oil

1 teaspoon salt

Prepare the polenta according to the package directions, adding olive oil and salt to the water. When the polenta is cooked, pour it into a lightly greased 12 by 17-inch sheet pan and smooth evenly. Let rest 20 minutes to firm up. Then using a 3-inch round cutter or stack cylinder, cut out the rounds to be used in your recipe.

Note: Experiment with different cut-out shapes: squares, triangles, ovals, etc. Polenta rounds make easy platforms for free-form stacks.

Polenta Variations

To the basic polenta add

• Butter and Parmesan cheese

• Rosemary and Gorgonzola cheese

• Italian herbs and Parmesan cheese

• Wild mushrooms sautéed in butter

• Caramelized onions and chives

• Roasted garlic

• Sundried tomatoes, diced

Risotto

YIELD: 3 CUPS

5 cups chicken stock (page 161)

4 tablespoons butter

1 onion, chopped

1 clove garlic, minced

1^1/$_2$ cups arborio rice

1 teaspoon salt

Freshly ground black pepper to taste

^{1}/$_2$ cup freshly grated Parmesan cheese (optional)

Heat the chicken stock to a simmer. In a large saucepan melt 2 tablespoons butter and sauté the onion and garlic until limp but not brown. Add the rice and stir to coat. Add ^{1}/$_2$ cup hot chicken stock and stir, allowing the rice to absorb all of the liquid. Cook the rice for 18 minutes, adding ^{1}/$_2$ cup of stock at a time, stirring until it is absorbed before adding more. (You may not need all of the hot stock.) Remove from the heat and stir in the additional 2 tablespoons butter, salt, pepper, and Parmesan.

Risotto Additions

• Strong cheeses, such as Asiago, aged Parmesan, pecorino, or Gorgonzola

• Fresh herbs

• Diced vegetables added with the onion

• Diced tomato added with chopped fresh basil at the end of cooking

• Chopped seafood added toward the end of cooking

• Chopped spinach and toasted pine nuts added at the end of cooking

Savory Crepes

YIELD: 40 3-INCH CREPES

3 large eggs

1 cup milk

$^1/_2$ cup water

4 tablespoons melted butter

1 cup all-purpose flour

$^1/_2$ teaspoon salt

$^1/_2$ cup clarified butter (page 161)

Mix the eggs, milk, water, melted butter, flour, and salt in a food processor until well blended. Let sit 1 hour, covered, in the refrigerator.

To make 3-inch crepes suitable for stacks, heat a small crepe pan over medium-high heat. Brush the pan lightly with clarified butter and, using a $1^1/_2$-ounce ladle, pour batter into the hot pan. Allow the crepe to cook until the edges begin to look dry and the top bubbles begin to break. Flip the crepe over and cook another 30 seconds.

Transfer the crepe to a plate and continue to cook remaining crepes, brushing the pan with butter as needed.

Crepes can be made ahead, stacked between layers of waxed paper, wrapped in plastic wrap, and frozen.

Note: Try using different herbs, seasonings, and nuts in crepe batter for an unusual taste.

Dessert Crepes

YIELD: 20 TO 25 LARGE CREPES OR 40 SMALLER ONES

4 eggs

1 cup all-purpose flour, sifted

2 tablespoons sugar

1 cup whole milk

$^1/_4$ cup water

$1^1/_2$ tablespoons melted butter

2 teaspoons vanilla

$^1/_2$ cup clarified butter (page 161)

Combine the eggs, flour, sugar, milk, water, melted butter, and vanilla in a food processor and blend 1 minute. Scrape down the sides and blend 15 seconds longer. Refrigerate 1 to 2 hours.

To make 3-inch crepes suitable for stacks, heat a small crepe pan over medium-high heat. Brush the pan lightly with clarified butter and, using a $1^1/_2$-ounce ladle, pour batter into the hot pan. Allow the crepe to cook until the edges begin to dry and the top bubbles begin to break. Flip the crepe over and cook an additional 30 seconds.

Transfer the crepe to a plate and continue cooking crepes until all the batter is used, brushing the pan with clarified butter as needed.

Crepes can be made ahead, stacked between layers of waxed paper, wrapped in plastic wrap, and frozen.

Note: Try the addition of split and scraped vanilla beans, ground toasted almonds or walnuts, or sweet seasonings such as cinnamon, nutmeg, allspice, or cardamom, for a different flavor.

Bread Pudding

YIELD: ABOUT 7 CUPS

A yummy base for dessert stacks—this is a basic recipe you can go wild with. Try adding chocolate, nuts, dried fruits, chocolate-covered English toffee, plums, peaches, apricots, or roasted apples. Make the bread pudding and layer with any of the above. Add interesting flavorings and sauces to complement. Also see the Stacks Matrix (page 8) for flavor pairings and ideas.

12 slices day-old country-style bread or pannetone

$1/_2$ cup sweet butter, room temperature

2 cups milk

$1^1/_2$ cups heavy whipping cream

6 egg yolks

$3/_4$ cup sugar

2 teaspoons vanilla

Pinch of salt

$1/_8$ teaspoon freshly ground nutmeg

Butter the bread and tear into 1-inch cubes (you should have about 5 cups). Place in a large bowl. Heat the milk and cream to simmering. Beat the egg yolks with the sugar and vanilla. Add the salt and nutmeg. Whisk the milk and cream into the egg yolks until well blended and smooth. Pour this custard over the bread and let stand for 45 minutes.

Preheat oven to 325°. Butter an 8-cup ovenproof dish. Pour in the bread pudding and bake in a water bath (see Note) for 1 hour, or until a knife inserted comes out clean. Serve warm.

Cool the pudding. Cut into rounds and slice each shape into 2 or 3 layers.

Note: A water bath or bain-marie is a method of cooking custards gently and evenly. Prepare a water bath by placing the dish you have prepared inside a larger pan. Fill the pan with hot water until it measures halfway up the sides of the inside pan. Bake as directed.

Pound Cake

YIELD: 2 LARGE POUND CAKES

$1^1/_2$ cups sweet butter, room temperature

1 (8-ounce) package cream cheese, room temperature

3 cups sugar

$1/_4$ cup freshly squeezed lemon juice

$1^1/_2$ tablespoons vanilla

1 tablespoon grated lemon zest

6 large eggs

3 cups all-purpose flour

$1/_4$ teaspoon salt

Preheat the oven to 350°. Lightly grease 2 large loaf pans. With an electric mixer, cream together the butter and cream cheese until fluffy. Add the sugar and beat 2 to 3 minutes. Add the lemon juice, vanilla, and zest. Beat well. Add the eggs, one at a time, beating well after each addition. Add the flour and salt and blend until smooth. Pour into prepared pans and bake for $1^1/_2$ hours or until a cake tester inserted in the center comes out clean. Cool in pan for 10 minutes, then turn out onto a rack and cool.

The Fab's Brownies

YIELD: 12 LARGE BROWNIES

Brownies are a great choice for stacks. Their density helps hold the stack together. Cut prepared brownies into layers. Then layer with your favorite fillings, nuts, fruits, and creams, in stack cylinders. Refer to the Stacks Matrix (page 8) for ideas.

1 cup sweet butter

1 cup unsweetened chocolate, broken into pieces

1 cup sugar

2 cups brown sugar

5 eggs

1 tablespoon vanilla

$1/_4$ teaspoon salt

1 cup all-purpose flour

$2/_3$ cup cake flour

$1/_2$ teaspoon baking powder

Preheat the oven to 375°.

Grease a 9 by 13-inch pan. Melt the butter and chocolate together in a double boiler. Set aside to cool.

Beat the sugar, brown sugar, eggs, and vanilla until fluffy, about 5 minutes. Stir in the cool chocolate. Mix together the salt, flour, cake flour, and baking powder. Mix together the chocolate mixture and flour until just combined. Pour into the prepared pan and bake until a crust forms and a toothpick comes out with a few moist crumbs, about 25 to 30 minutes. (The batter should not coat the toothpick. If it does, return the brownies to the oven for 2 to 5 minutes. Test again for doneness.) Cool completely.

Chocolate Sauce

YIELD: $1 1/_2$ CUPS

6 tablespoons sweet butter

$1 1/_2$ cups brown sugar

$1/_2$ cup superfine sugar

1 cup heavy whipping cream

Pinch of salt

4 tablespoons cocoa

2 teaspoons instant espresso powder

1 teaspoon vanilla extract

Heat the butter in a large saucepan. Stir in the sugar and brown sugar and allow to dissolve. Stir in the cream, salt, cocoa, and espresso. Bring to a simmer and cook for 5 minutes, whisking to blend. Remove from the heat and stir in the vanilla.

Can be stored, covered, in a glass container in the refrigerator for 1 month. Heat gently before using.

Chocolate–Peanut Butter Sauce

YIELD: ABOUT 1 $1/_2$ CUPS

2 tablespoons sweet butter

$1/_4$ cup packed dark brown sugar

2 tablespoons light corn syrup

$1/_2$ cup smooth peanut butter

$2/_3$ cup semisweet chocolate, cut into small pieces

$1/_2$ cup heavy whipping cream

1 teaspoon vanilla

Melt the butter in a saucepan and add the sugar and corn syrup. Stir until blended and bring to a boil. Add the peanut butter and chocolate and stir until melted and blended. Whisk in the cream and vanilla, lower the heat to a simmer, and simmer for 2 minutes. Cool.

The sauce can be stored in a glass container, covered, in the refrigerator for up to 1 month.

Orange Caramel Sauce

YIELD: 1 CUP

1 cup sugar

$1/_4$ cup water

$2/_3$ cup heavy whipping cream

3 tablespoons Cointreau (orange liqueur)

Place the sugar and water in a heavy saucepan and bring to a boil. Lower the heat to medium-high and cook, stirring occasionally until liquid turns a deep amber. Remove from the heat and very carefully stir in the cream. (It will bubble madly, just keep stirring!) Stir in the Cointreau.

The sauce can be stored in the refrigerator 1 to 2 weeks.

Note: To make classic caramel sauce, eliminate the Cointreau.

Resources

Cooking Supplies and Specialty Products

Bridge Kitchenware
214 East 52nd Street
New York, New York 10022
(212) 688-4220
fax: (212) 758-5387
www.bridgekitchenware.com
s.bridge@ix.netcom.com

The Culinary Institute of America at Greystone
2555 Main Street
St. Helena, California 94574
(888) 424-CHEF
fax: (877) 424-2433

Dean and DeLuca
Call or fax for locations and catalog.
(800) 221-7714
fax: (800) 781-4050
www.dean-deluca.com
WebHost@dean-deluca-catalog.com

Star Restaurant Equipment and Supply
6178 Sepulveda Blvd.
Van Nuys, California 91411
(818) 782-4460
fax: (818) 782-8179
www.starrestaurantequip.com

Surfas Gourmet Foods and Professional Cookware
8825 National Blvd.
Culver City, California 90232
(310) 559-4770
fax: (310) 559-4983

Sur La Table (catalog/merchandise)
(800) 243-0852
fax: (206) 682-1026
www.surlatable.com

1806 Fourth Street
Berkeley, California 94710
(510) 849-2252
fax: (510) 849-1980

161 West Colorado Blvd.
Pasadena, California 91105
(626) 744-9987
fax: (626) 744-9984

832 Avocado Avenue
Newport Beach, California 92660
(949) 640-0200
fax: (949) 640-2070

77 Maiden Lane
San Francisco, California 94108
(415) 732-7900
fax: (415) 732-7797

301 Wilshire Blvd.
Santa Monica, California 90401
(310) 395-0390
fax: (301) 395-5391

4050 East Thousand Oaks, Suite E
Thousand Oaks, California 91362
(805) 381-0030
fax: (805) 381-0040

4527 Travis Street, Suite A
Dallas, Texas 75205
(214) 219-4404
fax: (214) 219-3898

90 Central Way
Kirkland, Washington 98033
(425) 827-1311
fax: (425) 827-9561

84 Pine Street
Seattle, Washington 98101
(206) 448-2244
fax: (206) 448-2245

Sources for Stack Cylinders and Molds

The Art of Entertaining
Stack cylinders for this book by the author
(877) 4ASTACK
www.artofentertaining.com

Parrish's Cake Decorating Supply
225 West 146th Street
Gardena, California 90248
(310) 324-2253
fax: (310) 324-8277

See also:
Bridge Kitchenware
Culinary Institute of America at Greystone
Dean and DeLuca
Surfas Gourmet Food and Professional Cookware
Sur La Table

Specialty Food Products

Balducci's
424 Avenue of the Americas
New York, New York 10011
(800) BALDUCCI
www.balducci.com

Bristol Farms Market
Call for locations.
(310) 726-1300
www.bristolfarms.com

Ideal Cheese Shop Ltd.
1205 2nd Avenue
New York, New York 10021
(800) 382-0109
fax: (212) 223-1245
www.idealcheese.com
reblochon@idealcheese.com

Vivande Porta Via
2125 Fillmore Street
San Francisco, California 94115
(415) 346-4430

Zabar's Gourmet Foods
249 West 80th Street
New York, New York 10024
(212) 787-2000

See also:
Dean and DeLuca
Surfas Gourmet Foods and Professional Cookware

Asian Products

99 Ranch Markets
Call or visit website for locations.
(213) 625-3399
www.99ranch.com
custserv@99ranch.com

Cheese

Cheese Store of Beverly Hills (mail order)
419 North Beverly Drive
Beverly Hills, California 90210
(800) 547-1515 or (310) 278-2855
fax: (310) 278-3429
www.cheesestorebh.com
cheesestorebh@worldnet.att.net

Sonoma Cheese Factory
2 Spain Street
Sonoma, California 95476
(800) 535-2855
fax: (707) 996-1912
www.sonomacheese.com
scheese@napanet.net

See also:
Ideal Cheese Shop Ltd.

Chocolate

The Chocolate Catalogue
3983 Gratiot Street
St. Louis, Missouri 63110
(800) 325-8881 or (314) 534-2401
fax: (314) 534-2401

Fish, Caviar, and Seafood

Barney Greengrass, "Sturgeon King"
541 Amsterdam Avenue
New York, New York 10024
(212) 724-4707
fax: (212) 595-6565
www.nycfood.com/greengrass

Aristoff-Caviar and Fine Foods
321 North Robertson Blvd.
Los Angeles, California 90211
(800) 33ARISTOFF or (310) 271-6300
fax: (310) 271-8256
www.aristoff-caviar.com
info@aristoff-caviar.com

Jams, Jellies, Preserves, and Honey

American Spoon Foods
P.O. Box 566
Petoskey, Michigan 49770
(800) 222-5886
fax: (800) 647-9030
www.spoon.com
information@spoon.com

Sarabeth's Bakery
75 9th Avenue
New York, New York 10011
fax: (212) 996-6400
www.sarabeth.com
info@sarabeth.com

Stonewall Kitchen
469 US Route 1
York, Maine 03909
(800) 207-JAMS
www.stonewallkitchen.com
info@stonewallkitchen.com

Oregon Apiaries (flavored honey)
P.O. Box 1078
Newberg, Oregon 97132
(800) 676-1078
www.oregonhoney.com
honeybee@teleport.net

INDEX